SEVEN FIGURE LIFE

Online Wealth Building Strategies

DANNY TSANG

Seven Figure Media LLC.
www.SevenFigureLife.com

ISBN: 0692603603
ISBN-13: 978-0692603604

DEDICATION

This book is dedicated to the most selfless people that I know, my parents, for all of their sacrifices to ensure that my sister and I had what we need to pursue happy and prosperous lives. For believing in me, even when I turned out to be wrong. For questioning me, even when I thought I had all the answers. For being the good-hearted people that I constantly strive to emulate.

To my wife, who has followed me down the rabbit hole time and time again, from moving halfway across the country, to quitting her job to join me in a learn-as-we-go experiment. For allowing me to express my creativity and turning our home into a construction zone every few months. For supporting me while asking the right questions. For unconditional love.

To my family and friends, for putting up with me and my inability to take anything seriously.

To my customers and day one supporters, for trusting me with their hard-earned money and precious time.

DISCLAIMER

This book was written with the intention of providing accurate information on the subjects covered. However, it should be understood that the author and the publisher is not providing legal, financial, tax, or any other professional advice. All content is for educational purposes only. All businesses and investing involve a certain degree of risk. Losses are always possible. The reader should consult with proper legal, tax, or financial professionals prior to applying any strategies and information contained in this book. The author and publisher specifically disclaim any liability that is incurred from using or applying any contents of this book.

CONTENTS

Introduction

This is an unprecedented time in history. We are living in the New Economy. Never before have we had so much opportunity literally in the palm of our hands. When I started my first business, I was a sophomore in high school. I spent around $300 buying cheap fashion watches from a local supplier, and sold them on the sidewalk from a folding table. When I took the business online later that year, my life would never be the same again. Since that time I've never had a 9 to 5 job. I've never set my alarm clock unless I'm traveling. I manage my businesses and investments from anywhere in the world. With the global reach of the internet and the innovative tools and resources now available, this unique lifestyle of freedom and prosperity is available to any entrepreneur with the desire and the work ethic to make it a reality.

Mediocrity

With formal education and the conditioning of the banking and financial services industries, we're taught to follow a set course throughout life. Our outdated education system was designed to create workers who will spend their lives trading hours for dollars. In our society, even decent jobs require a college degree. To play by the rules, we have to go to school and get into debt just for the privilege of finding work to pay off that debt. Unfortunately, the college degree has become the equivalent of a high school degree a generation ago, so people now get into even more debt and spend more time pursuing higher degrees just to stand out. Next comes more debt. You'll need a car to get to work, and eventually a house to live in. We're conditioned to work most of our lives to pay bills and hand over what's left to slowly build up a nest egg through 401Ks and IRAs. While the banks make a guaranteed cut from our contributions, we're taught to sit back and wait for that money to grow so that one day we may stop working and hope that the money doesn't run out. That is the sad state of mediocrity that society is in today. Those who follow the rules and do as they're told are following a life course based on survival. It is merely a system designed to help people get through life. Since you're reading this book, I don't think you just want to survive. You want to be able to thrive.

Build a Seven Figure Life

The Seven Figure Life is a freedom lifestyle that focuses on two principles. First is the creation of income-producing assets. Instead of working yourself to pay bills, these systems will eventually generate the income to do so on your behalf. The second aspect of a Seven Figure Life is time and location freedom. With the unique synergy of income producing assets, coupled with time and location freedom, this lifestyle allows you to live like the rich, regardless of your net worth. At the most basic level, the two things rich people have is disposable income and the time to enjoy it. An unemployed person has all the time in the world, but no means to do exciting things. On the flip side, a high-earning specialist has disposable income, but likely works long hours. Their pay may be high, but they are still trading their time for it. The key to achieving the Seven Figure Life is to invest your time in building income streams rather than perpetually trading it for dollars. Once you build income streams that surpass your expenses, you are free to do whatever you want with the rest of your time. Like the rich, you'll have disposable income and the time to enjoy it.

The beauty of this lifestyle is that you can live like you're rich even when you're still building your assets and not making a ton of money. When most people think about being rich, they think about expensive cars and big houses. Those things will come with time. More importantly, this lifestyle gives you priceless moments. I'm talking about little things like being able to go eat at your favorite place when it's not crowded because everyone is at work. Rich is being able to bring your kids to the park any time you wish and never missing a game or a recital. Rich is not worrying about staying up late and not caring if it's a weekday or a weekend. The time freedom and location freedom of this lifestyle gives you these intangible luxuries.

Unlike having a boss and a paycheck, the Seven Figure Life offers freedom in every sense of the word. You are free to decide how much money you will make by allocating your time and effort accordingly. You are free to decide where that work is to be performed. You are free to decide when you get to travel. Being able to control every aspect of your own destiny is the epitome of the entrepreneurial spirit.

Most of what you'll read in this book is a slap in the face of conventional wisdom. In every aspect of life, when you do things like the majority, you're on the quickest route to becoming average. Everybody knows the tired old advice that if you live below your means, pay off your debt and put what's left over into a mutual fund, then you have a shot at becoming a millionaire at some point in the future. However, if you take that route, 30-40 of your best years are spent commuting to and from work and on work itself, while living a "spend below your means" lifestyle. It's too safe. It's like playing only defense in a basketball game when your team is not even ahead. The bottom line is that to get ahead in this new digital economy, you need money-generating assets, and then your money needs to go to work for you. This book is about building systems that make more money than a 9-5, getting better than average returns on your investments, and doing it all in style from anywhere you want whether it's your home office or a 5-star hotel suite.

I hope that what I'm saying sounds exciting to you, because the Seven Figure Life was never this available to any other generation in history. We live in a unique time and the internet has really changed the way the world does business. Before the 2000s, very rarely would you see an average person build a business, grow it, and still have time to travel and do amazing things daily. Before the internet, most entrepreneurs started brick and mortar businesses. This meant that startup costs (and risk) was significantly higher and profit potential was significantly lower due to geographic restrictions. Worst of all, owners had to physically be there, at least during the growth years. Before the internet, people would depend on brokers for key data regarding stocks or real estate listings. Now it's just a few keystrokes or opening an app. Take full advantage of the age that we live in. There has never been a better time to build the life that you want and escape the rat race that you were taught to embrace.

A Commitment to Learning

In order to excel, you must make a new commitment to learning. This is very different than the learning that we did in school. School teaches you general knowledge. What you need to excel is *specialized* knowledge. Successful people take years to learn and become great at what they do, yet people often only see the fruits of that labor. Therefore they wrongfully assume that the person simply got lucky, or that they are privileged. People think that they can never become like those special few. But the truth is that the majority of millionaires are self-made. There are blueprints for success. I firmly believe that with anything in life, it is simply knowledge that separates the top 10% from everyone else. You know that saying, "it's not what you know, but who you know?" Let me complete that thought. It's not what you know, it's who you know that will teach you what you need to know.

The problem with learning things is that a lot of people don't even know what learning truly means. In school, most of the time it is regurgitation or learning how to pass tests. Outside of school, often people say, "I learn something new every day". No, not really. They probably heard something new or read something new, but they didn't really learn something new. There are three stages to learning and mastering any skill or subject matter. You only learn something when all three stages are completed. I promise you that if you go through all three stages, you can be successful at anything you want. You can do what you want to do and live the life that you want to live. On the next page we'll go through each of the three stages in detail.

Absorption

Application

Refinement

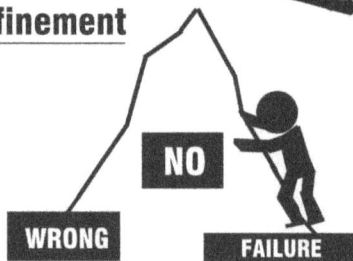

Absorption

The first stage is absorption. We live in a truly amazing era. We get to choose what we absorb and we have a world of choices too. Previous generations had television, radio, and printed media mostly from secondary sources. There was a filter between the primary source and end consumer (you). Now we have social media, blogs, online forums, books, and YouTube. You can find specialized knowledge directly from accomplished individuals from all over the world. Sadly, the majority of people out there never even reach this first stage. They believe that a formal education in school is all you need to succeed and thrive in the real world. They therefore never even pursue specialized knowledge. If you want to succeed, you must absorb specialized knowledge daily in the area that you are trying to learn and master.

Application

The second stage in the learning process is application. Of those people who have the desire to learn specialized skills, too many reach the first stage only to stop there. Some people are even crazy enough to think that absorption is the same thing as learning. They don't realize that there are multiple stages to learning and mastery. If I gave you a bunch of books about cars and engines, would you feel confident enough to open a mechanic shop? Of course not, because you haven't learned anything yet, you just absorbed it.

Then there are those who know that learning something doesn't stop at absorption, but they willingly let the knowledge sit "on the back burner". Bruce Lee once said, "knowledge is not enough, we must apply. Willing is not enough, we must do." There will be an inner dialog giving you all kinds of reasons why you shouldn't apply your new knowledge. There will be inner battles such as doubt and fear of failure as well as outside criticism. But the truth of the matter is that there is no time like the present. Anyone who became successful at anything was at one point a beginner, unsure of themselves. The key is that they did it anyway. Some people won't even finish this book. Some will finish it but let it sit then move on to the next book, then to the next CD series, etc.

Don't be one of those people. Apply what you absorb and lay your first brick knowing that eventually, through dedication and perseverance, you will have a castle.

Refinement

Most people don't even know that this stage exists in the learning process. They think that once they experience failure or rejection, it's over. They think that somehow the knowledge and information that they absorbed was wrong and that it doesn't work. On the contrary, the refinement stage is all about failure and setbacks. I'm willing to bet that the person who failed the most in anything, is the one who is the most successful at it. Basketball legend Michael Jordan has always attributed his success to his failures. Do you know why he's better at basketball than us? It's because he missed thousands upon thousands of more shots than we have. Body builders can lift heavier weights than us because they have failed over and over in the past. Never be afraid of failure or rejections.

A famous pastor once said that life is 10% what happens to you, and 90% how you react to it. This idea applies very well to the refinement stage of the learning process. Failing simply means you are given an opportunity to learn from mistakes. When you face rejections, you are given an opportunity to refine your proposition and do it again. Each time you are given that opportunity, you must pinpoint what didn't work, fix it, and try again. Thomas

Edison said that he failed 1000 times when he was inventing the light bulb. Could you imagine if he decided to give up during the first 10 or 100 iterations? There are only two ways that you can truly fail at something: you can fail if you quit, and you can fail by default if you never even try.

Only after you've gone through all three stages of the process completely have you actually learned something. Learning anything requires absorption, application and refinement. That's why it's so important that we lay this foundation before going forward into business and investing strategies and concepts. You'll be introduced to limitless possibilities, but it is up to you to apply and refine them when you're finished with this book.

3 Phase Journey To Wealth

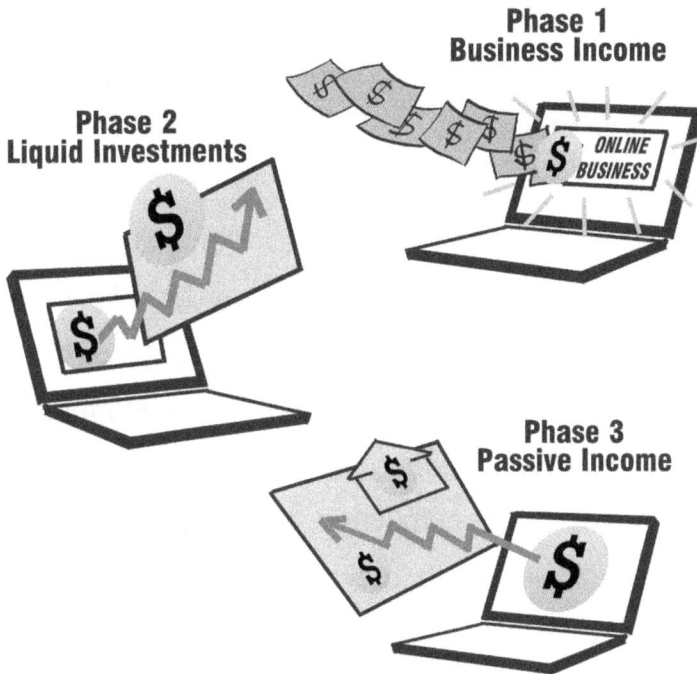

Phase 1
Business Income

Phase 2
Liquid Investments

ONLINE
BUSINESS

Phase 3
Passive Income

In the Seven Figure Life, wealth is built in three phases. The first phase of your journey is business income. This part of your journey involves investing your own time and energy into building and growing businesses that will give you perpetual streams of income well into the future. What you need to do is maximize this portion of your income to the best of your abilities while leveraging the abilities and expertise of others. With the amazing tools and resources available today, there couldn't be a better time to start or grow an online business. It takes real work, but once you get this income solid and stable, you can then implement ways to maintain that income while you personally spend less time on the business and move on to Phase 2.

You'll know it's time to move on to Phase 2 of the wealth journey when your primary businesses allow you to amass tens of thousands of dollars in savings that you simply don't know what to do with. When you feel you've already re-invested enough to grow the business, it is time to have the accumulated earnings work for you to accelerate your wealth growth. I call this phase liquid investments. While you can master the principles and strategies of any financial market, I focus primarily on the stock market because that's what worked for me. I'm not talking about buying some diversified mutual funds, then putting money in every month, hoping it keeps going up. That's how the average person invests. While it's better than nothing, I'm more interested in making real, solid profits that I can see. I strive to make hundreds and sometimes thousands for *each* short-term trade, while minimizing losses. That's how professional traders with specialized knowledge make a killing in the market while the average investor just blindly puts money into mutual funds. With these profits on top of your business income, your wealth begins to compound and grow like a snowball.

By the time you've mastered Phases 1 and 2, you'll want predictable, reliable passive income every month while you do close to nothing. You'll also want security for the money you've worked so hard to accumulate in all the previous years. Phase 3 is all about passive income through real estate acquisitions. It involves taking profits from business, stock trading and savings and storing it in high quality properties while collecting checks every month. This is what the wealthy have done for generations. You'll learn how to make real estate deals for short-term profits as well. As your property portfolio grows and so does your income, you can remove yourself more and more from your businesses and liquid investments, allowing you even more freedom. Your passive rental income will eventually match or surpass your business income. At this point you're likely already a millionaire and don't even care about that title anymore. You'll have financial freedom, the point where you only continue to work because you want to, not because you have to.

Journey to Wealth Phase 1: Business Income

Phase 1 of the Seven Figure Life wealth journey is quite simply the most important one. This is your foundation. Your business will pay for your living expenses and debt obligations so you can have enough left over to enjoy life and accumulate capital for the next phase. This phase determines whether you get to be an entrepreneur or an employee for the rest of your life. Invest the most time and effort here and it will pay off for the rest of your life.

Avoid Brick and Mortar

An online business is a low risk, high reward venture that you can run from anywhere, without a set schedule. Most brick and mortar businesses are the exact opposite. They require a much higher degree of financial risk with limited upside potential, while requiring your physical presence. Brick and mortar businesses often require set schedules and long hours. I have owned one brick and mortar business in my life and it was a restaurant during my college years. I call that arrangement owning a job. On paper, my partner and I were the owners, but in reality we just worked a physically demanding job that paid an average wage. The arrangement was a difficult one to deal with because if we spent all of our time there, we couldn't pursue other businesses, personal interests, or even our schoolwork. When we left the business in the hands of our employees, profits decreased drastically and payroll expenses increased drastically. No one hustles as hard as you will because you're the only one with skin in the game. So in order for the business to be profitable, usually the owner has to be present at least in the startup and growth years. I decided from then on that I would try to never get myself into that kind of arrangement again.

Generally there are three ways you get into a brick and mortar business. You can start the business from scratch, start a franchise, or purchase an existing business. All 3 scenarios include five or even six-figure startup costs that come out of your own pocket, either immediately or through debt. The first two scenarios put you deep in the red before you even get your first customer. The only thing that is guaranteed when you open your doors is your upcoming expenses. While internet businesses can be grown and operated entirely by freelancers and contractors, a brick and mortar business will usually require at least one full time employee from the get-go and more as the business grows. Compared to an online business, the financial risk involved in a brick and mortar business is absolutely astronomical.

Most brick and mortar startups fail due to insolvency within the first few years. This means that the revenue simply can't keep up with the fixed monthly expenses. For those that beat the odds and become one of the rare brick and mortar businesses that survive financially, the upside potential is still capped. Brick and mortar stores are limited to reaching an approximately 15-mile radius of customers. Then there is the issue of efficiency. Most brick and mortar businesses are inefficient because usually one employee serves one customer at any given time. More customers often requires more employees, which leaves you with not much of a net gain even with sales growth. Online businesses serve hundreds at a time and generate business 24 hours a day. So though you can *survive* with a brick and mortar business, you can *thrive* with the global reach of an online business.

While there are certainly plenty of successful brick and mortar businesses out there where the owners relax and their employees make them money, it wouldn't be a smart bet to hope and pray that it happens to you. If anything, a brick and mortar location should be used to supplement and solidify the branding of an existing business that you started online. After my restaurant venture, the only other time I opened a brick and mortar location was to supplement my existing, established jewelry business that already makes significant online income. Business and investing is a game of probability and risk to reward ratios. If you have a choice, you should always first put yourself into a scenario with low risk and high reward.

Many entrepreneurs like to say that they've failed their way to success. Remember that failing is a key stage in the learning process, and entrepreneurship is simply learning how to start and run a business. I've had many failed businesses, all of which turned into priceless lessons. I was able to push through all of them because they were low risk online businesses. Brick and mortar is a whole other story. I have a relative whose one single failed brick and mortar venture put his family into bankruptcy that they haven't recovered from to this day. You can't simply get up and try again or fail your way to success if one high risk deal wipes you out financially. This is why I talk about risk management and why I feel it is irresponsible for authors to only talk about the rainbows and butterflies of entrepreneurship while leaving out the risks and sacrifices that it requires.

Online Business Models

In the world of online businesses, there are many different companies, but most are based on one out of a handful of business models. When evaluating which business model to pursue, we will talk about three factors. First, we discuss the amount of financial risk involved. While some business models you can start for almost no money, others require thousands of dollars and then some. The second factor is potential. We often talk about risk to reward ratios. If the business is highly scalable with a potential to make a significant amount of money, we call that high reward. If there are challenges that'll cap the profit potential such as geographic restraints that brick and mortar stores face, then it would be considered low reward. The last factor we consider is the probability of success. Whatever that reward is, probability of success estimates the relative difficulty of reaching it and becoming profitable. In business and investing, it's best to find scenarios with low risk, high reward and a good probability of success. These ideal factors make the venture worthwhile. There are certain business models that I avoid and have struggled with. I later identified the problems with those models. Then there are those proven, sustainable and scalable business models that have been consistently profitable and can be easily replicated. Let's jump right into it.

Broker Model

In a broker model, your website is the middleman between the buyer and seller in a transaction. You do not stock any inventory. Some examples of these companies are Etsy and eBay. With this business model, you would set up a secure environment to conduct business and simply drive traffic to the website or app. Your platform would allow buyers and sellers to trade with one another. This model has been around since the beginning of the internet. While a few big names dominate the headlines, there are many smaller niche websites that specialize in everything from cars to watches. My good friend uses this business model in the baseball trading cards niche. The website generally makes money by charging sellers a fee, doing the payment processing for the transaction, or both.

In my early days, I launched an online jewelry auction site called Jewelbids.com. The site was very similar to eBay both in look and functionality, except for some reason I went with an ugly purple color scheme. The site and the technology were impressive, but the business model came with incredible challenges. The main problem with these types of businesses is that you need a sizable amount of traffic from the get-go and you need to sustain and grow that traffic throughout the life of the site. It's like a supermarket selling perishables like fruits and veggies. Once you start losing customers or you never get a large customer base to begin with, it's a downward spiral. It's all over. With the broker model, the startup phase is the most difficult because people can see how active the site is. If it's not an active site, people won't want to join to buy or sell. It's definitely a Catch-22 that is difficult to work around. You need a high number of members in order to generate business, but people are not willing to join in the first place because there aren't a high amount of members already there. Sellers don't bother to list on a site with low traffic, and buyers don't want to join a site with limited selection. With Jewelbids, I didn't gain enough traction even after spending a lot of my own money on ads, so I shut the site down after a few months and cut my losses.

The broker model is a high risk, high reward scenario with a low probability of success. If you make it, you'll enjoy income from fees while everyone else does the work. The business is infinitely scalable in theory. However, the chance of making it is low and the financial risk is high. These sites involve custom coding, app development, and heavy promotion from the get-go. I believe the only way to succeed with this business model is to be in a niche that is not yet dominated by a huge player. Not only that, you'll need real capital such as venture capitalist funding because the only chance of gaining traction is to have incredible technology (lots of talented people/employees) coupled with an enormous marketing and PR budget. Even tech giants such as Yahoo have failed with this business model. Yahoo Auctions was once a competitor to eBay. It never had enough traction to gain significant marketshare. If Yahoo couldn't make this model work, it definitely has a low probability of success for the startup entrepreneur. For these reasons, I do not recommend pursuing a business using the broker model.

I accepted this as a lesson learned in the refinement stage of the learning process. I realized that the idea was good, but the business model was flawed. By cutting losses, I didn't quit. I simply recognized the flaws with this model and moved on to others with my eyes still focused on the big picture.

Advertising Model

The advertising model has also been a timeless online business model. Many different businesses fall under this model. The idea is simple: you create a website or an app that attracts a huge following. With that reach, you can sell advertising to cover your expenses and to generate recurring income. This business model can be broken down further into two groups: a user-based advertising model and a content-based advertising model. The user-based model involves building up a user base that keeps coming back to the site or app. Some examples of a user-based ad model include big names like YouTube, Google, and Facebook. Content-based ad models depend on eyeballs only with less interaction from the viewers. Some examples include big names like Yahoo and GQ to smaller informational websites, some blogs and even social media accounts where the page owner with a big following sells advertising to brands.

This is a business model that I've tried on numerous occasions and didn't have much success with. While in college in the early 2000s, my partner and I launched a site using the user-based advertising business model. We invested a lot of money and time into a site that was called uTycoon.com. It was a Myspace-style social network developed for young entrepreneurs like ourselves. It was a niche social networking platform for like-minded individuals to connect on a more professional level than MySpace and Facebook. The site itself was incredible and the technology at the time was impressive. We had fully customizable profile pages. You were able to add associates and create groups just like the big name social networking sites. We had a forum with every category from business to investing. I was very proud of what we've built as our site and the logo was clean and beautiful. We had amazing freelance programmers. The site had all the ingredients of becoming what would eventually be Linkedin.

With decent PR and some media coverage, we got some traction but never did take off to a point where we would be highly profitable. The situation we were in was similar to the jewelry auction site, which was also dependent on a large user base and massive growth. We had an incredible looking platform, but we didn't grow fast enough. Because of that, not many people wanted to sign up and join what they could see was a "dead party". To keep investing money into PR, marketing and maintenance was like swinging a bat blindfolded and hoping that we will hit a grand slam. This was determined to be an unsustainable business model with little likelihood of generating a return for our money and time. My partner and I eventually shut the site down and parted ways.

Sometime after uTycoon, I built and launched a site called Real Estate Millionaires. Essentially it was an online forum catered to new real estate investors. It was populated by experienced real estate investors and newbies would be able to sign up ask questions for free. To get around the "dead party" problem and give users a reason to sign up, I paid experienced real estate investors from other popular forums to join and talk amongst one another. I had Google ads in strategic areas of the website. Over time, I discovered that the advertising dollars simply did not cover the cost to acquire new users. I also discovered that forum websites were resource-hungry, and hosting was very expensive at the time. Long story short, the numbers simply didn't make sense. Based on my projections at the time, the more the site grew the more money it would lose. Sure I could have waited to see if some rich venture capitalist would have bought the site, but that would once again be swinging the bat blindfolded. The only logical thing to do was to walk away from the business and move on.

To sum it all up, the user-based advertising model is high risk, high reward with a low probability of success. I get it: everyone wants to be the next Facebook or YouTube and everyone wants to make the next hot app. I've been there. However, most fail and you never ever hear about them. You only hear about the successful ones, which are a very tiny percentage of those entrepreneurs swinging for the fences with their own or someone else's money. Businesses that use this model often time require fully custom or semi-custom software platforms. It also means you'll have to develop an app that plays nicely across all the mobile platforms. You'll either need to convince highly skilled programmers to come on board for a percentage of the company, or you'll simply have to pay for their services. Quality work doesn't come cheap, and cheap work isn't good quality.

Assuming you get past the technology hurdle, it is difficult to make noise without a significant marketing budget or strong connections with the media, influencers or the industry you are serving. It is incredibly difficult to overcome all those challenges and become profitable. Some people will say, "shoot for the moon because even if you fail, you'll land on the stars." In this case, where you have high risk in addition to low probability of success, more often than not you'll just land on your face.

To get around the user base problem and high startup cost, my next venture using the advertising model was a relatively simple content-based website. Specifically, it was a magazine-style blog. In this case, I actually sold the site and rights to a new owner so I cannot disclose the specifics. It was essentially a personal finance website with free content. It was fully dependent on ads for income. I posted a lot and did earn some money. I topped out at about $1000 per month in ad revenue before I realized I was spending a significant amount of time writing. I ended up hiring a writer to supplement my own posts. That decreased my profit drastically since I had to pay the writer. If we stopped writing, viewership would decrease and so would the revenue. I was essentially trading my time for ad money, which was just like having a job. I spent so much time researching and writing, that I didn't have time to grow my other businesses or just enjoy my life. Eventually I had enough and sold the site to someone who didn't mind writing a lot.

The content-based advertising model is low risk, low reward, with a high probability of success. So while that sounds decent, with two favorable factors out of the three that we consider, the problem is the combo of high probability of success but low reward. It's cheap to start a content based website and host it these days. There's not much financial risk. And since hosting is so cheap, you can likely become profitable fast if you write a lot and spend a lot of time marketing your site using free methods. Surely the ads will generate enough clicks to cover the $10/mo. hosting right? The problem is you can only do so much in terms of writing, and in this business model, ad money requires eyeballs and eyeballs require lots of new, interesting, and high quality content. It is not a situation where you can do the work once and have it keep making money for you years into the future. This model is hard to scale to the point where you can make money without constantly being involved. So though the content-based advertising model is low risk, the low reward makes it not worth your while to pursue.

My Top Business Models

While trying to create a "next big thing" type of business, I discovered that online businesses using the broker model and the advertising models are risky and hard to make profitable. Luckily, while I was launching all these new businesses, my existing jewelry company was still profitable despite a lack of attention. After realizing that it was the business models themselves that were flawed in all those new ventures, I decided to re-focus on what had been working all along, e-commerce, and build on it. As my e-commerce businesses grew, I began receiving questions from family, friends and even customers about starting a business of their own. This led me to launch a new company, Seven Figure Media LLC, focused on teaching others how to start a business.

With this new venture, I am using the expert blog business model. While the e-commerce model involves selling mostly physical goods direct to customers, the expert blog model involves the sale of mostly digital goods direct to customers. The e-commerce model does not rely on a heavy initial user base, so you can grow your traffic and sales at any pace, without anyone noticing you are a new business. The expert blog model allows you to build a content-driven business without relying on ad money and the constant need to write. You simply create your product(s) or your sales copy one time and let it generate income for years. It does not rely on heavy traffic. In fact, it leverages the traffic you do have and maximizes the profits per visitor. These two business models have been consistently profitable for me, and either one would be a great choice for anyone looking to start a business today.

These two business models are not always low risk, high reward. Some people pursue e-commerce and blogging ventures with the wrong strategy, incurring unnecessary upfront risk. Then they execute their business in a manner that severely caps their growth potential and scalability. Remember, we want low risk and also high reward. After we go through an overview of each recommended business model, I will introduce you to my *strategies for success*. It is a blueprint, with step-by-step execution details that show you how to start these businesses with little money and maximize future profit potential. My strategies were developed directly from my 12+ years of experience. My businesses have generated millions of dollars in revenue and provide me with an extraordinary lifestyle. Let me be clear: I'm not saying everyone will succeed. However, what I am saying is that with low risk, high reward and a good probability of becoming profitable, you owe it to yourself to find out if you have what it takes to be a successful entrepreneur.

E-Commerce Model

E-commerce is synonymous with online business and it's not going away. In fact, it is still growing at a rapid pace and it is a primary reason for the decline of brick and mortar giants and malls in general. According to the US Commerce Department, web sales have experienced double-digit growth in nearly each of the past ten years. People have grown from acceptance to dependence on this way of doing business. From initial discovery, to research and purchasing, the entire sales process is done online for many new products that hit the market. E-commerce is what introduced me to the lifestyle I now enjoy. My first business involved selling watches on a makeshift table on the sidewalk in San Francisco. I was in high school so I could only do it on weekends. Though December was great due to gift shopping, most other weekends I only made a few hundred dollars standing there in the cold, talking to one person at a time. A few months later a friend of mine helped me with my first website made on Microsoft Frontpage, and the rest is history.

The types of items you can sell online are essentially limitless. I've seen anything from specialty socks to electric scooters sold through a website. I've personally purchased everything from live plants and aquatic life to a Jacuzzi tub during a home remodel, all on the internet. You can make your products, purchase them, or consign them. Some people make their own jewelry and clothes. Some people build things like custom dog beds, carved wood iPhone cases, and picture frames. What's become more popular these days are consignment operations. People give you their goods for you to sell online and you take a cut. This is particularly popular in fashion and specifically high end luxury goods where buyers would trust a reputable consignment store rather than the owner selling it themselves as a private party. Perhaps the most traditional route however, is to purchase goods wholesale and resell at a higher price.

Typically with an e-commerce business model, you sell products directly to the customers. You open a PayPal account and a merchant account and accept payments directly from customers. You have to provide all pre-sale and post-sale customer service. This may involve email and toll-free phone service. Then your company is responsible for packing and shipping the items directly to the customer. You are also responsible for lost packages, late packages and ultimately returns and exchanges. This model involves basically all of the roles of a traditional retail store, but done electronically and through shipping. The e-commerce model is perhaps the oldest form of online business and it's never going away.

E-Commerce Strategies For Success

I've developed a set of strategies based on experience and brain storming with other successful online business owners. My goal is to give you a high probability of success with minimal risk. Too many authors and startup guides ignore risk and only focus on the upside. You should only go all-in on a business after a successful proof of concept stage. That way if one business doesn't work out, you still have the resources to try again. These are the same strategies that have worked for me. I run my e-commerce businesses with what I call a *branded boutique* approach. I started with drop shipping and now my company has moved on to in-house designs, high volume production, international product sourcing and selling wholesale.

If you're starting or growing an independent e-commerce business today, you should recognize that more than likely you won't become the next Amazon. While it is possible, I always go with what is probable. It's better to win at an attainable goal than to wish for an unreachable one. If you go with a flea market approach and try to carry everything under the sun, chances are you will fail. People sometimes think that if they open a store with a ton of categories and hundreds or even thousands of products, they can make a good enough sales rotation. In the very early days of the internet, this is how many people made money. As a matter of fact it is how they've grown to become big players today. But in this mature online retail environment, it will be very difficult to compete that way. With a flea market approach, your business will just be seen as another generic web store struggling to find an identity. When that happens, people will only look at price because you're not offering anything else. Competing on price is a competition that you simply will not win these days.

The Branded Boutique

The branded boutique approach is something that gives you a much higher chance of adoption and sustainable growth. The "small is the new big" concept is growing both online and offline. Younger buyers like to support small businesses with character and a story. Additionally, with the social media landscape and the growth of mobile browsing (currently at 40-50% of all online sales), I am now seeing that people are tired of information overload.

Think about it: when you buy something from Amazon, are you really looking at all 100+ results for that 1 type of item? Me, I just find the one with the best reviews and a decent price and go on with my day, especially if I'm buying on my mobile device. In the past it was good to have a deep selection of items to attract the masses, but nowadays it is better to have a cherry-picked selection, market those few items well, and leave out the others. I believe this de-cluttered approach is what people want going forward. There is so much information and choices out there these days that simply making a decision has become an annoying task. As crazy as it sounds, it's almost like you'll be providing a service by telling your customers what to buy.

These days branding is everything. If you don't have a brand, you have nothing. This goes beyond an imprinted name or a label. It requires you to create an image, a lifestyle, and a culture that your brand represents. To give yourself an advantage over the competition, the branded boutique approach requires you to put yourself out there and become the face or at least the spokesperson for your company. I know its difficult for some of you as it was for me, but in this competitive business space, you really need every advantage you can get. If possible, choose a product category that you care about and have some passion for. Learn as much about the product and industry as possible and be able to demonstrate that expertise or passion on social media and your marketing materials. Through trust, appreciation for your content and sheer likability, you have a much higher chance of gaining and growing a devoted customer base. Be yourself and allow your brand to be an extension of you. At the end of the day, people buy from other people.

Product Sourcing Strategy

Now let's talk about product sourcing. I highly recommend initially finding suppliers that provide drop shipping service. Drop shipping is when a wholesale distributor agrees to send items directly to your customers on your behalf. This minimizes your inventory risk and brings your startup costs to nearly nothing. It allows you to allocate your limited startup resources into marketing and branding. Another major benefit of this arrangement is that you can test the niche and product line you want to carry and see how much potential it has without investing a ton of money upfront. In my own journey, I've had 3 failed dropship-based websites. One that stands out is a dropship gift wine website. It was a horrible niche for me to get into. The shipping was almost the cost of the wine itself. At the time, no one was selling wine online so I thought I had a shot. However, the concept simply didn't make sense for buyers. I didn't get enough sales to make it worthwhile to grow the business, so I cut losses and got out. The losses were a few hundred dollars in ads and the time to build the site.

If I had been greedy and shortsighted when I launched the business, I would have wanted lower initial prices per bottle. If that were the case, I wouldn't have used a drop shipping arrangement. I would have driven up to Napa and negotiated a lower price per bottle than the dropship supplier. I would have ended up with a garage full of wines, thousands of dollars tied up, and no way to sell any of it. If I'd gotten myself into that situation, I would have likely ended up drinking all of it while I cried away my sorrows.

While on the subject of price, when it comes to drop shipping I like to implement a strategy that I call "price as if". When you use a dropshipper, it's usually more expensive than buying and stocking inventory in bulk. This is because the supplier has to process your tiny order with the same effort of processing a larger order. Some charge a dropship fee as well. This is normal and it is worth it. But rather than trying to be greedy with a high mark up, I would price items as if I were paying the lower price by pre-purchasing and stocking the inventory. I would come as close to my lowest priced competitor as possible because that's the only way you can accurately gauge the market during your proof of concept stage. When you price items this way, you won't miss a big opportunity just because you overpriced the items to begin with.

What To Sell? - My Top Rules

While you can sell anything under the sun on the internet these days, not all niches are best suited for an e-commerce store. There are certain types of products that will help you be more profitable and avoid challenges. Below are my top rules for evaluating potential products to sell.

1. Under $500 price with the sweet spot being around $150. Anything over $500 is a much more difficult sell. Another reason to avoid high-ticket products is because they invite a lot of potentially fraudulent orders. Nowadays, fraud is everywhere and it is only going to get worse. There is even a small group of cardholders themselves who are committing what we

call "friendly fraud", buying products themselves and claiming it was unauthorized. Also, the more expensive the item is, the more service is expected before, during, and after the sale. That means phone service, call centers etc. I'd rather reply to emails at the beach.

2. Items should not be too big or fragile. You don't want the shipping cost to tack on an additional 20% to the cost of the item, which is what some heavy and bulky items may do. Shipping costs and materials are only going to rise as time goes on, so it is best to prepare for that going in. Another big problem is when something goes wrong with the shipment or the product, you're forced to pay for return shipping as well.

3. Avoid universally searchable items. What I mean by this is anything with an SKU, a model number etc. I'm sure we've all done this. You go to a website or a store, you see something, then you search Google by model number or SKU for whoever is cheaper by $5 and buy from them instead. Don't put your business in the position where people can easily price shop. The beauty of the jewelry business is that no one knows

what something is truly supposed to cost. Even when we sell branded watches such as Invicta, I purposely do not list the SKU of the item. We go by pictures and description only, making it more difficult for buyers to find the dozens of fly-by-night sellers who are willing to slash prices for a quick buck while providing virtually no customer service.

4. Avoid fads. You don't want to build an entire business dedicated to Tomagotchis or Pogs (remember those?). Years back, I knew someone who invested heavily in an entire e-commerce business selling everything that has to do with mini-discs. He sold players, burners, actual discs, everything. After the mini-disc format itself failed, so did the business. Tens of thousands of dollars were lost. You need to go with something that will stand the test of time.

    To get an idea of "big picture" trends in your potential niche, use the Google trend tool at www.google.com/trends. Type in 4-6 keywords or product names related to your target niche and just look at the overall graph. You don't want to get into something that has a steep dive in interest or something that doesn't have much interest (search volume) to begin with.

5. Avoid one-and-done items aka slash-and-burn items. These are items that are one-offs. If you're buying or making works of art made with natural rocks or something along the same lines, where each one is different from the last, then you're setting yourself up for so much unnecessary work. Imagine taking pictures, adding titles and descriptions for every single item that you sell. It is difficult to scale a business like that. It would be more of a hobby than a business. The beauty of the internet is that you can do something one time and have it keep selling for you for years. Don't lose that advantage if you don't have to.

Where to Sell Your Items

Selling channels are far and vast these days, with private websites being the leading channel and third party platforms eBay, Amazon and Etsy next. Your primary focus should always be your own e-commerce website. That is the one asset which you have full control over and true ownership of. All of your marketing efforts will not only get you sales, but add value to the website when it comes time to sell your business. Usually, people get the itch to sell solely on third party platforms like Amazon or eBay for two reasons: they either believe it is more profitable because these platforms readily provide traffic, or they think building and growing their own website is too difficult. When you sell on a third party website, you're still paying for the traffic in the form of fees after the sale. So it's just a question of whether you want to pre-pay for traffic or pay afterward.

Relying solely on a third party selling platform is a bad idea because you wouldn't be building your brand that way. You'd actually be working your butt off to build *their* brand. You'll become another faceless seller among the thousands of search results. Because of this, the only way sellers stand out is to offer free shipping and to slash profits further in what I call an epic race to the bottom. Sellers will often undercut each other even if it's 25 cents at a time. When this kind of behavior takes place, it benefits the website you are selling on and their customers. That is exactly what they want. You as a seller are merely a pawn used to source products and drive prices (and profit margins) down while the platform's popularity and profits grow. Secondly, as a seller on a third party site, you don't own anything. You will be putting in hours, months and years into building something on what is essentially just rented land. That means you are at the mercy of the powers that be when it comes to fee hikes, search algorithm changes, suspension, and selling limitations.

About a decade ago, a good friend of mine had his eBay account suspended indefinitely after some policy changes. This happened after he spent years building up a power seller account that generated tens of thousands of dollars in monthly profits. It was a profitable sales channel, and out of nowhere, the rug was pulled out from under him and he had absolutely no way to change the decision. After much frustration, he retooled and focused on growing his website and is now doing better than ever, doing millions of dollars in sales each year without a third party platform taking a cut. However, a lot of profit was lost during the immediate aftermath of the suspension. He should have been focusing on the website in the first place. It was an expensive lesson, but the good thing is that it happened sooner rather than later.

3rd Party Platform Strategy

After hearing some of the horror stories, you may be thinking that I'm against selling on eBay, Amazon, Esty, etc. That is not the case. I'm going to show you how to do so in a way where you use them for your benefit and not the other way around. Your website should be your primary selling channel. All outside channels should act as additional streams of both income and website traffic which over time will grow both your sales and your brand. Whenever my items are sold on third party sites, we market our brand. While many platforms have rules against linking to your website, nowhere does it say you can't mention the brand of the item (your brand) in the title or description. Right in the item description I put our logo and a mini "our story" type paragraph. Whether customers immediately buy or not, that means eyeballs on your brand. Business is a game of inches and when you add up all those inches, that is the difference between success and failure. The primary goal of selling on outside channels is to take advantage of what the third party platforms provide, and that is primarily traffic and thus attention.

The best marketing opportunities happen after the sale. In the past I've asked a drop shipper to include my fliers, which offer a discount code for future purchases on our website. I encourage customers to join our newsletter and follow us on social media for a chance to win prizes and gift certificates. The sale itself should serve as access to that customer's attention, allowing you to cultivate the relationship and build future sales. eBay sale confirmation emails often includes the buyer's user name and email address next to it. PayPal confirmation emails contain an email address as well. You can add these emails to your email marketing software, which will then send out an automated email urging that person to join your newsletter. Another way to benefit from a third party website sale is to take advantage of the concept of reciprocity. This means that after the sale, you surprise your customer with something unexpected, and your customer feels a psychological need to return a favor to your brand. Ideas include sending free related samples, free related accessories, a handwritten thank-you card etc., along with a note to asking them to join your newsletter, tell their friends about your brand, or follow you on social media.

Product Strategy for 3rd Party Platform

Since a lot of third party selling platforms are price sensitive, I wouldn't dilute my brand by heavily discounting prices just to pick up some sales. Once you cut prices too much, it's hard to go back. On the flip side, as I mentioned before it's hard to stand out on these third party sites unless you've got great prices. This leads to my product strategy for third party platforms, which is the use of closeout items. During the early stages of my jewelry brands, I would purchase closeout or liquidation goods from suppliers at dirt-cheap prices. Often the price was lower than even what they originally paid for the goods. They simply wanted to get rid of the stuff because they only had a few left or they were no longer making those styles. I would make sure that the items were in the same overall product category or a related category, but not part of the core product line itself. What I would do is take some quick pictures and throw them up on eBay with the starting bid price being my break-even point including postage, fees and time. No one knows what a closeout item would look like compared to an item at full retail. To a customer, it just looks like an amazing deal. Most suppliers have close outs readily available. All you have to do is ask and make a deal.

After the sale I'd send a thank-you letter and a flier with a discount code. I did this for tens of thousands of transactions over the years. I knew my strategy worked because I would see website orders come in with that discount code applied. I would also send new customers automated emails encouraging them to join our newsletter list. You'll notice that I mention the newsletter list a lot and I talk about how the real marketing opportunity presents itself after that initial sale. The reason is because it is much easier to advertise to someone who has already purchased from you versus someone who doesn't know who you are. A lot of your profits will be from repeat customers and their circle. That is why building an email list from the get-go is so important.

Now think about this. Since your closeout items are sold at break-even pricing but you get the attention of a willing buyer, you are essentially getting *free advertising* while building up your newsletter subscribers and getting products into the hands of future customers. With these strategies, you are using the third party platforms to your advantage and not the other way around. You are using their traffic to grow *your* website and *your* brand.

Maximizing Profits

As your primary e-commerce website continues to grow, you have firmly achieved proof of concept. You know that you're getting sales and your customer base is growing. Now is the time to invest in proven products at lower prices so you can make more money. I use the word *invest* because you now have a probable and foreseeable return on investment. If you purchased product and stocked it from the get-go, you would have been taking an unnecessary risk because you didn't know how hard it would be to sell. After the proof of concept stage, the best thing to do is to take your top 10 bestselling products and start stocking the items in bulk and shipping the goods yourself. Research and negotiate the best possible pricing. Never pay the asking price on a wholesale catalog or supplier website. Most likely there are quantity price breaks if you call or meet the company in person. During this stage of the business you should be confident on what is selling in a stable manner and your goal is to extract more profit out of those proven products. Most stores generate the majority of their revenue from solid long-term performers. This is called the 80/20 rule and it applies to many aspects of business and life. Roughly 20% of the products will produce 80% of the profits. 20% of your advertising will produce 80% of the sale conversions. Your goal is to find out what the 20% is and focus on that to maximize profits.

The Student Becomes the Teacher

The next phase is not possible for all product niches, so when choosing what to sell online, try to also pick a type of product that you can apply the following strategy to.

Once you have a good understanding of what sells and what your audience wants, the best way to really multiply profits and truly establish yourself as a brand is to manufacture and produce your own line of in-house products based on proven sellers. Outsourced manufacturers are now easy to find online and the whole transaction can be set up from anywhere in the world. You can use your creativity, add your own signature touches and even add features that do not exist in the market. By releasing your own line, you are not only increasing the profits even more from existing retail sales, you'll be opening up a world of new revenue possibilities. When you can buy goods at similar prices that your suppliers pay, you can begin to wholesale your line to brick and mortar stores. You can even start drop shipping for other online sellers as well. At this point, you are no longer just your previous suppliers' customer, but a competitor as well. When my own jewelry line Jewelure.com begins to offer drop shipping for the first time in 2016, I expect our sales volume to at least double after the initial launch. The added volume would give me more negotiation leverage, leading to better pricing with our factories. This forms a cycle of higher profit at every distribution level that you control, such as manufacturing, wholesale and retail. In business, this tactic is known as *vertical integration.*

Get Started

So there you have it. With my e-commerce strategies for success, you can start and grow your own branded online store with big potential using very little money. These are the same strategies I have used to start my jewelry brands and grow them into a multi-million dollar business. If starting an e-commerce business sounds exciting to you, go to my blog SevenFigureLife.com now. I offer a FREE email training course on e-commerce that will give you step-by-step, detailed instructions on establishing your brand, finding drop ship suppliers, and setting up your store. It is entirely possible to get set up and get your first sale within *weeks.* Visit the site and get the free email course today.

Expert Blog Business Model

The expert blog model is another business model that has been consistently profitable for me, and is therefore my second recommended business model. Aside from physical goods, many individuals make an amazing living selling digital and informational products on websites and blogs. These entrepreneurs build a following by essentially offering solutions to problems. Specialized knowledge or passion in a unique area can be turned into products and thus profits. There are many people who make six and even seven figures a year by dedicating themselves to learning and becoming go-to people in their respective niches. They demonstrate their expertise through content marketing, then they sell information or educational courses to their visitors and fans. These are not necessarily celebrities or people with special degrees or certifications. These are normal people who work hard to perfect their craft while consistently marketing themselves and their respective brands. I promise you that anyone can become an expert on anything, so don't let that word scare you away from this profitable business model.

This is a business model that is low risk, and high reward with a good probability of success. It is incredibly scalable and if you become successful at it, you can generate perpetual income from anywhere. We'll now go over all of the different ways to generate revenue from a blog. Then we'll follow up again with my *strategies for success*, which provides the best game plan in pursuing this type of business if you so choose.

In-House Digital Products

In-house digital products are products that you create yourself and sell through your website. These products have the largest profit margins. You do the work once, and sell it over and over at virtually no new added cost. An example is what you're looking at right now - unless you're old school and bought the paperback! Most likely you paid about $20 and you downloaded this book. This is one of my in-house digital products. I also have in-house digital products that sell for $149 - $499. These products can range from free mini-guides, to higher ticket items such as professionally produced video lessons and specific training packages that go well beyond the scope of a book. Higher ticket products typically cost a few hundred dollars. You can even create a subscription-based product and have customers pay you monthly for on-going information or a series of lessons. I've even seen seminars and international masterminds serve as top-level in-house products that cost thousands. The possibilities and potential for these products is only limited by your imagination and amount of dedication.

Services

People with both specialized knowledge as well as specialized skill can build a blog business around the services that they offer. For example, web designers, SEO specialists, photographers and video editors can all sell their products as well as their services online and reach a worldwide audience. On their website, they can offer Photoshop courses or mini courses on branding and online marketing for free or at a low price point, which gives them a nice stream of income. More importantly, the mini courses and in-house digital products create an authority/expert image that will produce revenue for their service offerings. Think about this. Would you want your website designed by some random freelancer, or the guy who literally wrote the book on web design and created a thriving brand for himself? That's how it'll appear to potential customers.

In another example of this unique synergy, the fitness world has been turned upside down with the wide acceptance of online coaching. Fitness professionals now offer meal plans and workout plans online at a lower rate than at their brick and mortar full time locations. With an affordable price and worldwide reach, it's no wonder some fitness enthusiasts make over $10,000 a month just from their websites alone. Many of them use a subscription-based model which gives them income month after month. You see, internet businesses are all about leverage. You can create a product and sales page once, and it'll sell your product or service for years to come. With subscription-based products, the sales page does the selling once, and the income keeps growing with time.

Affiliate Marketing

Another major income generator that expert bloggers utilize is affiliate marketing. In this arrangement, you sell digital goods, subscriptions and sometimes even physical goods without any of those items being your own. You would sign up with the publisher, seller or affiliate network and get your own personalized link to the product. You would put those links on blog posts, email newsletters, social media or your Youtube channel to promote someone else's product or service that is related to your niche. When someone clicks that link, they are taken to the website of the product provider. If your customer purchases something, you get an agreed-upon commission split. You don't deal with any pre- or post-sale customer service. You are not the one accepting the customer's payment and you are not delivering the products. Everything happens behind the scenes and you'll earn a portion of the sale (usually 30-50%) afterward. It's straightforward and the concept has been around as long as the internet itself. Generally, highly competitive and common products will have a lower commission. The big money is in those niche digital products that require more selling than just a few sentences and a link. Successful affiliate marketers leverage their authority, influence and brand in order to recommend products they truly believe in that are also highly profitable. This allows you to profit from products that you didn't even have to create!

The best part about affiliate marketing is that you have a vast array of products that are already at your disposal. You can create accounts with some of the most popular affiliate networks such as Linkshare (linkshare.com), CJ (cj.com), click bank (clickbank.com), and Share a Sale (shareasale.com). Within each network you will see a ton of product offerings. You can see how well each product performs, the amount of commission it pays and the current popularity of the product. Right off the bat you can filter the search results to find the most popular and profitable products in your niche. How great is that? When you create your own product, it takes time and money and you don't know how the public will respond. It can be a hit or miss. You also have to be responsible 100% for the closing of the sale whereas with affiliate products you do a bit of marketing to promote the product but the sale is closed by the creator of the product. Again, you can see the stats that will give you an idea of the product's conversion rates and popularity beforehand so you know which creators are best at closing the sale. There are always new products and you have the freedom to promote whichever ones you want on any given day. This gives you timeless money generating opportunities once you have a good following.

The downside to affiliate marketing is of course the commission split. You don't make all of the money whereas with your own product, you sell it yourself and you keep all of the proceeds. Another often-overlooked downside to traditional affiliate marketing is that you essentially send your customer or reader away through banners and links. Imagine owning a restaurant. The customer sees your restaurant from across the street. She is attracted to it, so she comes in to look at the menu. After the customer takes a seat, you recommend the taco truck across the street and send her there so you get a commission. While you didn't have to cook or clean up in order to get that commission, you run the risk of that customer never coming back because she realizes that the tacos taste better than your food! With affiliate marketing, you have to send your customers to someone else's site to close the deal. You only get paid if they buy someone else's product. In short, your customer has turned into their customer, at least for the moment. You may not lose the customer for good, but at the very least, the lifetime value of that customer will decrease because their money, attention and loyalty will be divided up even more than it already was. Because of this, you don't want to rely solely on affiliate marketing in the long run.

Reporter Vs. Expert Blog

I want to take a moment to note the difference between a reporter style blog and the expert blog model that we're talking about. You may be thinking, hey, didn't you mention earlier in the book that a blog isn't a good business model? Let me clarify. A typical blogger is like a reporter. They are someone or a group of people that writes blog posts on various topics such as celebrity gossip, fashion, cars, smartphones, internet marketing, etc. When someone is simply a reporter, they often default to using the advertising model that I described in an earlier chapter. These blogs are designed to attract readers en masse and keep them coming back for fresh content. The goal is to have so much traffic that they can make significant amounts of money from advertising alone. For established sites that already have a following, or the blogs written by famous people, that model is fine because they can generate a ton of traffic. The advertising dollars will be enough to pay for writers to keep pumping out content, which will maintain and grow the readership further.

For individuals, startups and not yet famous people, the ad based blogging model may have worked 10 years ago, but today it would be very difficult to build up and sustain a large readership. Today, everyone's attention span is lower and information overload is everywhere. To try and build up the amount of consistent traffic needed to make good money purely from ads would not be the best use of your resources. Consider the following: for an individual whose blog does not offer a solution that can solve readers' problems, it is basically just a glorified Facebook page. You share stories and write opinions, but no matter how much time you spend making it look nice, it is forgettable. Not only that, but you need to pump out a ridiculous amount of fresh content just to maintain the existing readership, let alone grow it. I'm not saying it's impossible for you to blog about some obscure topic and get big, but the odds are stacked against you.

The expert blog model is a self-contained moneymaker, just like an e-commerce website that sells physical products. Many are built on a blogging platform such as Wordpress, but the idea is not to have fresh news daily and then covering the site with ads. It's more about quality over quantity. The website itself would already offer solutions to a problem, such as educational courses, e-books, cook books, etc. The blog section of the website is used to further market those core products by writing about the niche, general updates, news in your industry etc. You will always be indirectly selling, not just attracting attention for ads. With this model you do not need the vast amount of traffic like an ad-dependent blog because you will make more profit per visitor. The advertising model pays you pennies per visitor. With an expert blog model, you can do quite well with a moderate amount of loyal fans by selling them more products as time goes on.

Expert Blog Strategies for Success

If you believe you have passion for a particular subject, you can turn it into a profitable online business that you can run from anywhere in the world. This model gives you even more location freedom than the e-commerce model since there are usually no physical products involved. In my entrepreneurial journey, I've built successful e-commerce businesses that ship physical products, so naturally I created a new business to teach others how to do the same. My blog SevenFigureLife.com is set up using an expert blog business model. It allows me to make money by teaching others how to make money online. Though a lot of content I give away for free, the money is made through the sale of digital products and one time or passive recurring affiliate income. I initially worked on this project part time but it has now grown into its own brand. My products consist of digital guides and even a physical luxury accessories line under the brand Seven Figure. I'm going to show you strategies that will allow you to do the same with very little money and highly scalable profit potential. This is a low risk, high reward business model with a good probability of success.

Get The Ball Rolling

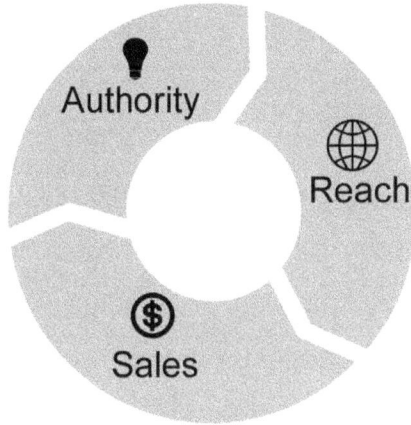

To become successful with this business model, the three primary ingredients you need are authority, reach and sales. These elements go hand-in-hand and, over time, create a snowball effect that can massively scale your business. The more you demonstrate expertise (authority) through free content, the more reach you will have as other websites link back to you. That reach naturally leads to sales. The first batch of sales then increases your authority and your conversion rates because you can show testimonials, case studies and reviews to new customers. As you build more authority through reviews, case studies and testimonials, more media outlets will be willing to take you seriously and feature you and your website. With that increased exposure, your reach obviously grows and — guess what? your authority and sales also grow because you can then leverage that media coverage. By showing your new customers that you have testimonials, case studies, reviews, and now even serious media coverage, your sales conversions will be at their highest level ever while your traffic is at its highest level ever. Talk about perfect timing. I know your head is probably spinning. This massive synergy effect is the reason why successful entrepreneurs make 6 and 7 figure annual incomes from their blogs. No matter what you do, remember that every action you take, every bit of work you put into your business should either increase your reach or your authority. Sales will follow. Don't waste time on anything else. You want to get this snowball rolling as soon as possible.

How to Gain Authority

To gain authority in a niche, you generally need to be an expert on it, but you don't necessarily need to be the best expert. You may be thinking that you're not an expert on any subject or you don't know about a subject well enough where you can sell information. The word expert might even intimidate you. First off, I want to remind you that everyone started somewhere. Every single person who operates one of these businesses is a student themselves who's constantly perfecting not only their writing and sales skills but also constantly learning new things within the niche. They sign up for similar websites' newsletters and read articles written by their peers. They read books, join forums, watch Youtube videos on the subject and they listen to podcasts. There's nothing new under the sun. If you spend the time to absorb a wide range of information, then form your own opinions and strategies, you can eventually develop your own digital products and sell them. Secondly, authority doesn't necessarily mean you need stratospheric expert status. It just means that you need to know something that someone else wants to know. I'm not Jeff Bezos, founder of Amazon, but I'll teach you how to build a profitable e-commerce business that'll help you build wealth and give you time and location freedom. You simply have to solve a problem at a price people are willing to pay. It's that simple.

Choosing a Topic

Before you think to yourself that you need to go out and learn something new to become an expert, you should take some time to brainstorm on your existing skill set, work life, and interests. Try to think of every aspect of your personal and professional life and see if you can come up with creative or unique knowledge that you can turn into a product and sell. Remember that you should also have a passion for the topic because you will be writing on and researching it for years. The possibilities are endless. I've seen people selling courses on playing piano, tennis lessons, golf swings, foreign languages, hair cutting, landscaping, pond-building, jewelry making and more. Are you good at public speaking? Become an expert on that and sell courses. Are you good at door to door sales? Develop a course to help others. Are you just a confident and happy person? Yes, build a business around helping others become like you. I know someone who makes thousands of dollars a month simply by helping others become more confident.

Over fifteen years ago I bought a book by Carole Maggio. She's an expert on facial exercises and I happened to be looking for exactly that. At some point between then and now, she built the website Facercise.com and it utilizes this business model very well. In another example, I recently began to research laundromats because I'm considering purchasing a few of them in my area. The *problem* was I didn't know much about laundromat valuations and operations. The *solution* was that I bought books and training material from current laundromat owners who turned their knowledge into sellable products.

As you can see with these examples, the possibilities are endless. What makes these people experts, you ask? It's simple. They know more than me on the topic, so to me, they are experts. I don't care about what college they went to or if they even went to college at all. I don't care about professional certifications and licenses because anyone can take some courses and pass a test. I care if they can solve my problem at a price I'm willing to pay. That's all there is to it in this business.

Brainstorming topics from your current experiences and interests is one of the hardest parts for people, so let me give you some more examples of how a bit of specialized knowledge can turn into a business. The obvious example is myself. For over twelve years, my primary income was from my e-commerce websites. The income and freedom has given me an amazing lifestyle. I never planned on teaching others, but when you absorb so much information and try everything that doesn't work, you end up with what does work and that information is worth something to someone. Who would want to waste time and money sorting through the information jungle, trying and failing when they can just get proven strategies upfront from someone who has done it?

Here's another example for a great topic. My longtime friend opened a barbershop when we got out of college. He boot-strapped it, and my guess is it only cost a few thousand dollars to start, if that. He now has multiple locations and has also founded a barber college. He makes money from tuition, the haircuts that the public pays during training at the college, and post graduation when some students end up renting a spot from one of his shops. The amount of income streams generated from what was once just one neighborhood barbershop is staggering. If my friend built an expert blog business around the topic of opening your own barbershop, he has instant authority, expertise, and an amazing story. What if he spent a few months to create a powerful course that explains exactly how to replicate his business model? It would include everything from starting your first shop with as little money as possible, to cost-effective marketing and eventually building passive income from renting out individual chairs. If I were an aspiring barber or stylist, I would pay gladly pay around $500 for the course without blinking an eye. Many people would because it would easily pay for itself. After all, we pay a lot more for college courses on material we will never use again for the rest of our lives. If he sells just <u>one guide</u> per day, which is a conservative number when we are reaching a worldwide audience, that is a $182,500 annual income from one single product.

Another method for finding a suitable topic is to dig deeper into one of the dominant topics to create your niche. The dominant topics are health and fitness, money and investing, fashion, and consumer goods. You don't want to have a topic too broad within these topics because it would be hard to stand out. However, you can dig a little deeper to differentiate yourself. Let's say you want to write about cars, but you're not going to compete with Motortrend. You could narrow your focus to write only about classic Ford Mustangs. That can lead to products about restoration and affiliate marketing for physical goods related to those cars. A friend of mine operates a health and wellness blog. Within that niche, she specifically writes about Filipino vegan cooking. So the next time I want to create a meatless version of my favorite Filipino dish, she is the go-to person. I literally do not know any other person in her niche. She has done joint ventures with restaurants, appeared in various media and television shows, sold sauces and is preparing to release a cookbook and other products. In my case, there are many bloggers that talk about making money online, but I specifically specialize in low risk, high reward models with a high probability of success. I believe that the majority of people who are looking to start an online business want something that they can start with very little money but has the potential for big profits over time. That is how I differentiate myself.

Finding The Sweet Spot

As you can see from the many examples I have showed you, the ideal topic for an expert blog business would be one that fits in the sweet spot between knowledge that is too common and knowledge so specialized that no one will care. A good way to pick up topic ideas is to visit the magazine aisle at your local bookstore. You will see all kinds of topics. These publishers have invested time and money to research the niche and build a readership. Take advantage of the research that they have already paid for. If it's an extremely esoteric topic, you can get an idea of how popular it is by calling or emailing the magazine as a potential advertiser and ask them about their circulation numbers and how long they have been around. You'll be surprised how many entrepreneurs still generate ideas from the magazine aisle.

Build Your Email List

The Most Effective Post Pregnancy Fat Burning Exercises

Sign up for your free copy of our revolutionary e-book filled
with the best exercises from the leading experts in fitness

Email Address

SIGN UP NOW

The email opt-in box pictured above is something that you will commonly see on nearly all expert blog websites and even e-commerce stores, because the owners now realize the power of email. From the moment you start this business, your objective is to start building your email list. In the earlier days of blogs and personal websites, most people tried to drive as much traffic as possible to their websites in order to increase ad revenue. As it turns out, that isn't building a business, that is simply getting yourself another job. You had to keep replenishing those visitors who would click the ads and leave your site, sometimes never to return. While those advertisers got the sale and the customer's post-sale attention, you were left with a much smaller portion of the lifetime value of that lead. When you build an email list, you are essentially building up a digital venue to house your audience. You can take this venue with you at any time and you can reach your audience through a medium that is still highly reliable. People may stop checking their Facebook or twitter. A social network can be the hottest one year and dead the next. You can't "take" those fans and followers with you like you can with an email list. People will always have an email address for serious life matters like bills, receipts, business communications, and even password recoveries for nearly all of their outside accounts. Email gives you direct access to eyeballs now and for the foreseeable future.

Once a customer is in your list, you have their attention just as long as they don't unsubscribe. During this time, which can be years and years, you will offer those subscribers valuable and helpful content and updates. You want to make it as easy as possible for your readers to receive your content. These days it is all about convenience. Think of it as takeout vs. free delivery. A customer who doesn't have to go through the hassle of coming to you will be a happier customer. Without an email list, even your most dedicated readers and fans will get busy and stop checking your site. Eventually, they may even forget about you. Subtle email communication from you is the best way to stay fresh in their minds.

Aside from updates and content, you will also generate revenue from these emails by promoting products and services. I use the 80/20 rule when it comes to selling through email. I offer valuable content for free 80% of the time and I only sell a maximum of 20% of the time.

One special note regarding affiliate products: you want to make sure that you understand everything about a product before recommending it. Never recommend something based on the commission rate alone because your reputation is more important than a few big sales when you are building a true long-term sustainable business. For example, when you sign up for the SevenFigureLife.com newsletter, I actually use the vast majority of products or services I recommend. This business model is like any other that sells digital or physical goods. A long-term satisfied customer is much more valuable than a quick sale.

The Sales Funnel

TRAFFIC

OFFER

WEBSITE — Quality content to attract new customers (free)

EMAIL SIGN-UP — Product given to new customer in exchange for email signup. (free)

ENTRY LEVEL PRODUCT — Entry level ($20 - $50) product offered to newsletter subscribers. Add value for customer. Designed to be paired with or related to initial free product.

PREMIUM PRODUCTS — Premium high end comprehensive training ($200 - $2000) and subscription based services that add value for the customer ($20 - $200/mo.) Live Events ($300 - $3000)

CONSULTING — Mentorship and private coaching for your most dedicated customers ($5000+) Followed up with private consultations ($100-$200/) hr

The sales funnel is an automated selling machine that primarily utilizes the power of email marketing. Conceptually, it is a road that each of your customers is placed on in order for you to maximize their lifetime profit potential. It is shaped like a funnel because generally you will have some customers that drop off and do not go on to the next phase. As time goes on, the customers will make purchases at progressively higher prices, ultimately leaving your most dedicated readers, followers, and customers purchasing your high-ticket premium products. As new customers enter the funnel at different times, this long-term sales approach is designed to create a dynamic revenue strategy that becomes more profitable the longer you're in business. It is designed to go to work for you and generate revenue 24/7. I use sales funnels to generate the vast majority of the revenue from my blog. Book sales are a small portion of the overall revenue picture.

At the very top of the sales funnel is the discovery process. This is the start of the selling process. You are selling potential customers the idea that your blog is offering them something of value in the topic that you're covering. You will attract traffic by offering free high quality content. This content is on your own website as well as outside platforms such as guest posting on related websites, social media, Youtube videos, interviews and other outside promotion and networking.

When those customers become readers of your website, the next step is to convince them to sign up to your email newsletter. The majority of high-earning bloggers create something of value and offer it for free in exchange for an email signup. Usually it is an e-book or a guide of some sort. For fitness bloggers, it can be an e-book of the "top 5 exercises to get lean in 30 days". For food bloggers, it can be an e-book containing "My most popular 10 minute recipes". If you're selling courses on being confident, the ebook may be "How to increase sales by becoming more confident." The possibilities are vast and only limited by your imagination. This is the second sale that is made in the funnel. At this point you are selling the customers on the idea that your free item is worth their time and effort to enter their email and sign up for it. That being said, no matter how good you are at selling, not all visitors will sign up. Thus, conceptually the funnel becomes narrower.

Once the customer signs up, they are emailed the free product for their enjoyment. The freebie item serves three purposes. While the primary job is to attract people to sign up for your newsletter, it is also meant to demonstrate your knowledge and expertise in the subject. Lastly, the purpose of the freebie item is to truly help your reader in some way. With the last two goals achieved, you build rapport and credibility with the customer. They will be happy and willing to receive more information from you. Over time, you will follow up with periodic emails to keep your customer informed, to educate and ultimately to sell products that cost real dollars.

Your emails should eventually lead to the introduction of an entry-level product. These are often in the $20 - $50 range that you create yourself. It can be another more comprehensive e-book, a video learning series or something of that nature. The possibilities are endless. This could be a product that you are already offering for sale on your site, but at this point you would link to it and explain how the customer would benefit from it. The chances of converting someone in the funnel is much higher than a stranger stumbling onto the sales page online.

Some people will buy your entry-level product and some people will not buy. Some will buy at a later time. The funnel continues to become narrower with time. Those who do buy your product will oftentimes become a long term supporter, assuming your product does what it says. Usually, a portion of these former customers will then continue to buy more of your products and they would be willing to spend more money. This happens because they already know you, they trust you and your previous products have helped them. Because it is much easier to sell to existing customers, you can introduce higher cost premium products further down the line, say weeks or even months after the initial signup. These are items that cost anywhere from $200 to thousands of dollars depending on what niche you are in and what type of product or service you are offering.

High cost premium products offer your customers a lot more value than a simple e-book. Often times these are comprehensive training packages that contain various modules and step-by-step instruction. It could be a video training series, and it could even mean private coaching. It depends on your subject and how far you want to take it. I know what you're thinking. At this point you have no idea how to create a high-ticket premium product. You don't believe someone will pay $500+ for something you create. It sounds complex, technical, expensive and time consuming. Don't worry, most successful expert blog owners started off thinking the same thing, including myself. There is a much easier way to help you get started with your blog and making big ticket sales without having to develop your own product.

Leverage The Authority of Others

When it comes to the higher ticket products and subscription services, do not create your own when you're just getting started. A daunting task like that will drain you in creativity, focus, time and money. It can cost a lot of money to produce high quality digital products. When you first start out, you don't have a lot of authority and reach, so the odds of converting your own expensive product are not good. This is why my strategy calls for selling someone else's high ticket products related to your topic. Through affiliate networks such as click bank, you can sell other publishers' products in the hundreds of dollars range and make anywhere from 30-60% of that as a commission per sale.

Selling other peoples' products allow you to leverage *their* existing authority. The product already exists; you can see testimonials, see their professional sales page, and get an idea of how well it converts from the stats. As I mentioned earlier, do thorough research to make sure that the high-ticket product you recommend to your customers is actually a good product. While you sell other peoples' products, this buys you time to develop your own signature high-ticket product slowly. With this time you can continue to learn more things, which can eventually become material for your product.

Some blogging pros will tell you that affiliate marketing is no good as it leads the customer away from you and allows them to become someone else's customer.

Essentially it is like punching a hole in your sales funnel. That is only true in basic affiliate marketing where you plaster banner ads and affiliate links all over your site, each offering low-cost products. The visitor may never even sign up for your newsletter — instead, they are led away by an affiliate link. With my strategy, you create your own low priced entry-level product and you only push the higher ticket affiliate products later down the funnel. At that point, the customer is already towards the bottom of the funnel, reaching their maximum profit potential. You already have their attention and trust. Selling other publishers' products won't hurt you at that point in the funnel. As a matter of fact, you can sell different products at different times, which essentially means you are increasing your product selection and possibility of profits.

Utilizing affiliate marketing to sell to existing customers is like utilizing a dropship arrangement, which I talked about when covering the e-commerce business model. In the beginning, you want to use your time and money wisely because you may be short on both. Marketing is the most important part of a startup, so it's best to minimize the upfront investment in products and leave fulfillment to someone who is already doing it well. Just like an e-commerce business, you can slowly cut ties with suppliers, or in this case, third party publishers. As you gain more reach and authority, you can experiment with creating more of your own in-house digital products in various price ranges and multiply your revenue overnight.

Create Recurring Income

At some point in the sales funnel, you'll want to find and offer subscription-based products. This could be a service related to the topic, or oftentimes education and information. There are many of these services that offer on-going commissions, meaning you get that same commission percentage as long as the customer's subscription remains active. This part of your sales funnel is essential because it creates passive income that you can grow with time. This is money that keeps coming in even if you stop working completely. Over the course of years, it can turn into significant dollar amounts. Currently, my sales funnels promote to my readers three to five trusted services that I actually use myself on a daily basis. They are subscription-based, so I receive on-going monthly payments from these companies. The amounts will actually grow with time without me having to do anything besides setting up the initial sales emails.

Get Started

By utilizing my strategies for success, you can get started in the blogging business today. The expert blog business model is completely scalable and once your reach and authority is strong, your income channels are vast and highly profitable. It is the perfect business to start and grow on the side at a very low cost, while still giving you the potential for massive income. If you want to start your own expert blog business quickly and easily, sign up for my free email course on my website. The course is more in-depth than this book and it provides step-by-step instruction on how to create and design the blog itself and how to develop a sales funnel. These are the exact same steps I've taken to build my highly profitable blog business. I'll show you how to build a self-contained selling machine of your very own. Sign up for the FREE course. There's a link to the blog business course on my website www.SevenFigureLife.com.

Journey To Wealth Phase 2:
Liquid Investments

In Phase 1 of the journey to wealth, it's all about building online businesses to create steady streams of income. While having business income will already give you a lifestyle with excellent time and location freedom, it should be combined with good investments. Business income and investments work together to create a powerful synergy to increase the velocity of wealth building. While Phase 1 is all about you working to build income streams, Phase 2 is all about that money going to work for you. Learning as much as possible about investing is important for two reasons. The first is that as entrepreneurs, we don't have any type of pension plan, so-called benefits or employer matches. Our only retirement plan is what we build. Therefore you must learn money-generating and passive income tools outside of the business itself. Secondly, there is way too much misinformation out there coming from the very financial services industry that is supposed to help us. For the most part, the industry exists to help itself.

For Phase 2 in the journey to wealth, my primary investment vehicle is the stock market. It fits in so well with the Seven Figure Life philosophy of time and location freedom. Previous generations relied on brokers for information and placing orders. Now you can research and invest from anywhere with an internet connection. Powerful charting software that was once reserved for pros is now readily available for retail consumers. With stocks and ETFs, there are a vast amount of tools and resources available and all are accessible online. Another major benefit of investing in stocks is the fact that the stock market is highly liquid. This allows you to get out of positions to both lock-in profits or minimize losses in a matter of seconds. Later in the book, I'll explain why liquidity is extremely important in Phase 2 as opposed to something illiquid like investing in real estate.

Buy and Hold vs. Trading

There are two fundamental methodologies when it comes to investing in the stock market. There are those who are strictly buy-and-hold investors. They are in it for the long haul. They will devote a certain amount of their earnings into a 401K or an IRA, and even complex and often unnecessary financial instruments like whole life insurance. These accounts are usually comprised of a diversified portfolio of different funds, stocks and other securities. The investors will periodically contribute more money into their portfolio. They are looking at holding the same securities for years and even decades. They will ride out the dips and they will hold on when prices soar. The goal is to amass a large nest egg by the time they decide to retire and hope that those funds last for the rest of their lives. It is a hands-off approach to investing. Most people fall into this category of investor because this is pushed by many in the financial services industry.

The second type of investors are shorter term momentum traders. Traders profit on the foreseeable swings in stock prices. The one thing that is certain is that stock prices go up and they go down. These people want to buy low, sell high, or sell high and buy low (short selling). Their goal is to amass a large nest egg *before* they retire as well as generate income. This type of investing requires much more education and skill. It is more of a hands-on approach at dealing with your finances and your future.

Which is Better?

There is no quantitative proof as to which is a better methodology for everyone. You can only decide which way is best for you. The buy-and-hold investing strategy is more hands-off. It is an inactive approach. Though every now and then the portfolio will be re-balanced, for the most part it is a "set it and forget it" strategy. If the prices of securities are up one month, the investor's portfolio makes money. If prices go down, it loses. The hope is that in the long term, the prices keep going up to infinity and you do not decide to retire during a down cycle, or what's known as a *bear market*. It is a single-dimensional strategy that only makes money with increasing share prices.

Traders on the other hand are proactive in the market and continuously learning and perfecting their skills. They read charts, digest the latest economic news from around the world, and find opportunities in any market. They will buy at certain price levels, called entry points. They will sell when it reaches certain exit points. They will short a stock when they believe the price is overextended, in other words bet against it. They will even set up trades where they make money when the market goes sideways! The primary difference is that trading tools are multi-dimensional, allowing traders to position themselves to profit in any price direction, and in any market.

Mutual Funds

Mutual funds are investment products that are primarily used in the buy-and-hold, long term investing methodology. Most funds do not short stocks, meaning that they only make you money when the shares that they hold go up in value. They are products designed to make profits for the mutual fund company through guaranteed on-going fees paid for by the investors (you). Mutual fund companies are very clever in their marketing. They take advantage of people's desire to have something come easy. The notion is that you can simply hand your money over to a professional fund manager and they'll pick and choose what to buy for you. You don't have to do anything except buy shares of that particular mutual fund. They will advertise their best performing funds at the moment. Once the fund starts to perform poorly or even take losses long enough, you'll never hear of that fund again and they'll be promoting another one. Many financial advisors are merely salespeople that receive a commission when they sell you shares of a mutual fund.

The facts are that mutual funds are notorious for two things: Most have high fees and most of them underperform. When you invest your money into a mutual fund, you're responsible for ongoing fees such as the management fee which goes to hiring the actual fund manager, administrative costs and an on-going 12B-1 fee which pays for brokerage commissions and the fund's marketing costs. Yep, you pay for them to market themselves to get more customers even though it doesn't help the performance of your investment at all. In total, these fees range from maybe 1.5% - 2%. To the average person, it doesn't sound like a lot of money. You wouldn't know it, but by the time you retire, you'll only end up with a fraction of what you *should have* accumulated. The reason is because you're not just losing those small percentages in fees alone, but those fees cause a major slowdown of the snowball-like effect of compounding that your money experiences over time. You lose the opportunity cost of those fees, which should have been invested over the long run. To add insult to injury, you pay all those fees to managers that make millions of dollars a year, and the majority of those fund managers can't even keep up with the general stock market over the long run. The benchmark S&P 500 has returned 7.30% (excluding dividends) in annualized returns from Jan 1990 to Dec 31 2014. I read that over 90% of mutual funds can't even match the S&P 500. They underperform and they get paid no matter what. Must be nice.

How to Reduce Fees

If I were to settle for the hands-off, buy-and-hold strategy at some point in my life, I would do it the much smarter way. Nowadays there are many online brokerages or even new free services like WiseBanyan.com, which builds you a diversified portfolio based on low cost ETFs and index funds that simply track benchmarks such as the S&P 500, the Dow Jones Industrial Average, certain sectors, or commodities such as gold and silver. This way you can be diversified and utilize the buy and hold strategy and at least you're not paying high fees for a mutual fund that robs you slowly. You're buying instruments that mimic the performance of the general market, the same market benchmarks that most fund managers can't even beat over the long run anyway. Low fees would be the best bet for those who believe in the hands-off, buy-and-hold strategy.

While avoiding high cost mutual funds and reducing fees would help your portfolio simply by keeping more of your money invested, it doesn't protect you from big losses. There is a fundamental flaw with the long-term buy-and-hold methodology, especially now. When you buy and hold for the long term, you are betting on the stock market to rise in perpetuity. You are hoping that it'll go up forever and that your money is safe from pro-longed bear markets. This is the main reason that at this moment, I have no interest in parking large sums of money into a long-term buy-an-hold account and hoping that those two things hold true in the long run. A brief look into the history of the stock market explains why I feel that way.

A History of The Stock Market

A long time ago, investing in the stock market was really just something that the wealthy did. The first time that stocks were introduced to the general public was in the 1920s, leading to widespread speculation by unsophisticated investors. This form of gambling was seen as a sure bet, much like buying real estate today. Because prices just kept going up, investors continued to buy overvalued stocks with borrowed money (on margin), which later resulted in the great crash of 1929. This set up the dominos that ultimately led to the Great Depression, a decade-long period of high unemployment and a poor economy. After World War 2, America's economy was going strong again. Unemployment was low and factories were busy. When it came to retirement, the average American worker relied on pension plans. Workers would transfer part of their income towards the fund and would later receive a guaranteed income stream during retirement. Most people didn't mix stock investments with retirement. The two were often seen as contrasting things. After all, pensions were much safer.

However, by 1974, Congress passed the Employees Retirement Income Security Act (ERISA), followed by the Revenue Act in 1978. These laws created a set of standards for retirement plans and started the rise in 401K plans and the demise of the safe, guaranteed income of pension plans. Due to the 401K, most average employees are in the stock market these days whether they like it or not. As the saying goes, it was the only game in town. Starting in the 80s, a fresh new wave of unsophisticated investors entered the stock market, much like what had happened right before the great crash of 1929 and the Great Depression.

S&P 500
1950-2012

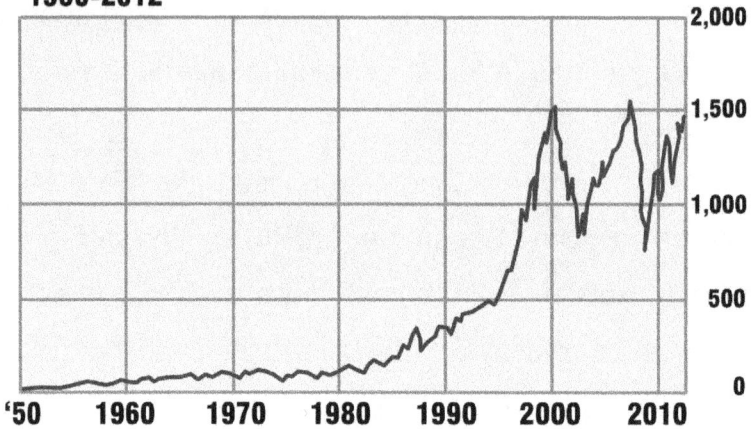

Source: Standard & Poor's

Look at the above chart of the S&P 500. The S&P 500 represents 500 large companies that are listed in the New York Stock exchange or the Nasdaq. This index, along with the Dow Jones Industrial Average index, provides a snapshot of stock prices in the overall US market. As you can see from the chart, stock prices rose slowly and naturally before the 1980s. By the mid 80s, 401K plans were adopted by many large companies and you can see the prices start rising a lot more dramatically than before 401K plans came onto the scene. This is because of the massive influx of new investors, in the form of 401K plans. Average people began buying stocks and driving prices up. This phenomenon ushered in a period of un-natural growth in the markets.

By the mid 90s it was a full-blown casino. It was the 1920s all over again. Everyone from your mailman to your waiter saw people making money in stocks, so they started investing due to both greed and the fear of missing out on profits. This drove stocks to astronomical and unsustainable prices.

Artificial Demand

By looking back at this history, you can see that while companies did earn more and the economy did grow, the majority of stock price increases was simply due to more unsophisticated investors coming into the market. The masses that entered the market as a result of 401Ks and the gamblers and speculators that followed was a big reason that stocks rose disproportionally in the last three decades compared to any other time in history. Most people got into the market because there was no alternative (401K people), or they were looking to make a quick buck (speculators). By the early 2000s, sophisticated investors, aka the smart money, saw that the market was overextended and stock price valuations made no sense. The recognized that the artificial demand was unsustainable. They began to cash out and the market eventually crashed.

Government Intervention

You can see on the previous S&P 500 chart that after the sell-off in the early 2000s and the terrorist attacks on September 11th, stock prices were on their way down. This period was the market correcting itself. When this happened, the US government stepped in to prevent the correction from completing its course. They slashed interest rates and President Bush signed a stimulus package into law. With low interest rates, people didn't get much of a return for keeping money in CDs and savings accounts, so they began buying things and investing again. Stock prices rose. However, due to cheap money and loose lending policies, all those speculators started buying houses, effectively forming the housing bubble. Sub prime loans were re-packaged and sold as AAA grade securities on Wall Street. Come 2007, the housing market fell off a cliff and everything started falling apart when it became known that the re-packaged securities on Wall Street were worthless. The chain reaction caused almost a complete collapse of the global banking system in 2008. Once again, the government stepped in. They bailed out banks and corporations, purchased the bad securities and slashed interest rates. In other words, they were going to fix the problem with more of the elements that created the problem to begin with.

Government intervention makes our economy less of a free market. I do think that the actions came with good intentions. They didn't want retirees losing 30-40% of their life savings in a form of retirement plan that they helped to create. Also, the people in charge also wanted to protect their legacies. No politician in power wants to have the Great Depression repeat itself on his or her watch. After all, pictures still exist today showing the tents set up by unemployed homeless people in Central Park during the Great Depression under president Hoover. They show signs that read "Hooverville", which is what the locals called the area.

I believe that allowing the economy to go through recessions and corrections <u>completely</u> is the only way to truly cure what is wrong with it. Some poorly-managed companies need to fail, as do some banks who took unnecessary risks. Obviously they were not doing things correctly if they got themselves to the brink of bankruptcy to begin with. As of this writing, it doesn't look like government intervention is going to stop. It seems no one wants to taste the awful medicine that is required to fix the economy. Government intervention is not limited to the United States. China recently had some sell off in its stock market and a slowdown in their economy. They have just slashed interest rates and devalued their currency in an attempt to boost their economy and the stock market. They even halted trading on a day where the markets were tanking. Unfortunately, every time governments try to prop up the economy and the stock market with artificial demand, the bubble simply grows larger.

What Do You Think Will Happen?

Looking back at history, we can see what truly created the major run-ups in stock prices besides the natural growth of the economy. We know it was artificial demand. In the 1980s, stock prices rose significantly from the sheer number of new people that entered the market via retirement plans in a short amount of time. We know that in the 1990s, speculators joined the party and took prices to unprecedented levels. After the crash of 2000, we understand that it was government intervention with cheap money and low interest rates that caused stock prices to rise again. After the crash of 2008, we saw the Federal Reserve step in again to purchase bad securities, slash interest rates and generally assure the public that they will do whatever necessary to prop up the stock market. That signal from the Fed caused more artificial demand as large financial institutions and corporations simply used cheap borrowed money to buy stocks since they knew prices would only go up. The problem with artificial demand is that it runs out, and when it goes away it goes away quickly, especially as the bubble grows larger.

Currently, there is no "new" group of people that I can see entering the stock market to support these price levels. Millennials are bogged down with massive debt from the rising costs of education and living. They are suffering from the inflation that was caused by the massive government intervention and their printing of money in the recent decades. There's not much left to invest. Interest rates will inevitably rise. On top of that, the Baby Boomer generation is retiring and withdrawing their money from the stock market.

A Return to Natural Growth

I believe that at some point in the future, we will experience a phenomenon which I call a return to natural growth in stock prices and the economy. It will be a correction that wipes out the majority of the artificial demand that has been propping up the market. I believe that the boom and bust economy that the government has created is not sustainable and at some point even government intervention won't help. What happens when interest rates are already at 0 and there is still no growth in the economy? How can stock prices continue to go up at that point? If I am right, then there will be a crash in the stock market bigger than ever before. When that major correction happens, we will not see the drastic bounce back in stock prices because the government has already exhausted all their options. It is called a correction for a reason. I believe in the concept of a regression towards the mean. These crashes happen because the market is trying to correct itself and return to a state of natural growth. In recent times, the big corrections were stopped before the process was complete. The problem for the government is that if they allow the corrections to run their course, which is the right thing to do in the long run, then in the short run millions of people will lose a lot of money that they are depending on. It will most definitely cause a second Great Depression. Sadly, one day there will be no choice. We will reach a breaking point where a big correction is imminent and unstoppable. Personally, I don't have the stomach to watch a six or seven figure long-term portfolio lose 20-30% of its value in a matter of days. That is exactly what will happen to long-term buy-and-hold investors who do not study history and see the crash coming.

The Average investor

In summary, the average investor will buy and hold for the long term, in a diversified portfolio created by their online broker or financial advisor. They often invest in mutual funds, which contains numerous fees that suck money and decreases returns over the course of decades. In my opinion, they are also taking a big risk by having a buy-and-hold strategy with the possibility of the return to natural growth (big crash) occurring at some point in the future. That is my biggest concern with the whole buy-and-hold philosophy. However, even if a major crash doesn't happen in our investment lifetime, my problem with being an average investor is exactly that! — it's average! It is simply a strategy to keep up with inflation and survive. It is not a strategy to thrive. If you do what everyone else is doing and you're getting average returns, then by that logic you will have an average life and an average retirement, right?

I don't know about you, but average is not for me. That's why I equip myself with the most tools as possible to deal with any market condition and to profit from it. I am fully devoted to trading the stock market and having an active, hands-on approach to growing my wealth and creating the life and the retirement of my dreams, while taking care of my family and loved ones.

The Benefits of Trading

Aside from the risks and limited upside potential of the buy-and-hold methodology, perhaps it's more important to recognize the *benefits* of momentum trading. This investing philosophy is short term and designed to ride the waves of price momentum in any market direction. Many professional traders and successful moguls invest this way, especially in these unprecedented times of artificial demand, government intervention and boom and bust cycles. In a 2014 interview, billionaire Mark Cuban mentioned that he keeps a lot of his investment capital in cash and waits for opportunities rather than parking it in a buy-and-hold account. He is famous for saving his own fortune by foreseeing the dot com crash of the 2000s and setting up short term trades that allowed him to actually profit from the eventual collapse of the market. I invest the same way and you can too. When I see opportunities present themselves, I make the trade, get out at specific points, take my profits, and move on. If I see risks on the horizon, I re-think my positions or take precautionary measures. The primary difference between someone who does buy-and-hold and someone who trades on momentum is that the buy-and-hold person only makes money when the market goes up. It is a one-dimensional strategy. The educated and skilled momentum trader can make money in any market condition whether prices are going up, down or sideways. It is a multi-dimensional strategy.

Technical Analysis

Technical analysis a skill set that is used by most momentum traders. By studying chart patterns, we take relevant information from what the market has told us and what it is currently telling us, in order to formulate a high probability forecast of short term market direction. Nobody can tell the future in the long term, not the financial whiz on TV and certainly not your financial advisor. No one knows what a stock price will be in five years and your guess is just as good as theirs. The point of technical analysis is to simply get yourself into a position where you have high probability of being right in the short to medium term based on past patterns and real time information. In the following pages, we will go over some of the most basic and fundamental principles of technical analysis. I have skipped the complex and exotic chart patterns in order to focus on timeless fundamental ones.

Support and Resistance

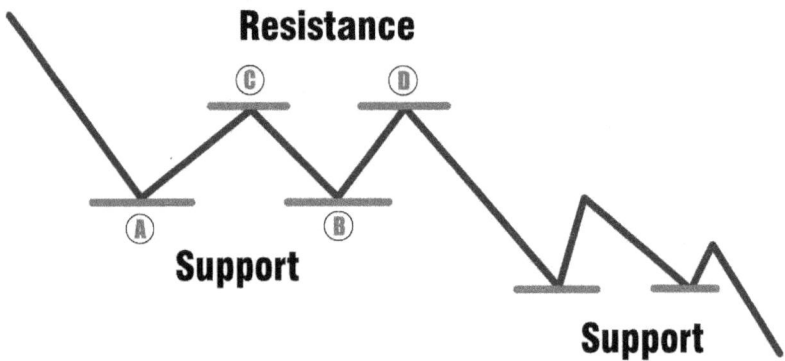

Support and resistance are the most basic principles in technical analysis. Look at the simple stock chart above. Points A and B are what is as known as support. Support is a general price level where the value of an asset stops to further decline. They are price levels where investors think the stock is a bargain and start to buy and drive the price back up. Points C and D is known as resistance. Resistance is a general price level where historically, the value of an asset fails to push through when the price is trending up. This is when investors start to think that the stock is overvalued. New buyers are no longer purchasing and existing shareholders start to sell off and take profits. The price starts to fall. Generally, the more often support and resistance levels occurs in the past, the more reliable they are considered going forward. For example, point B is reliable because point A was a proven support level in the past.

Support Becomes Resistance

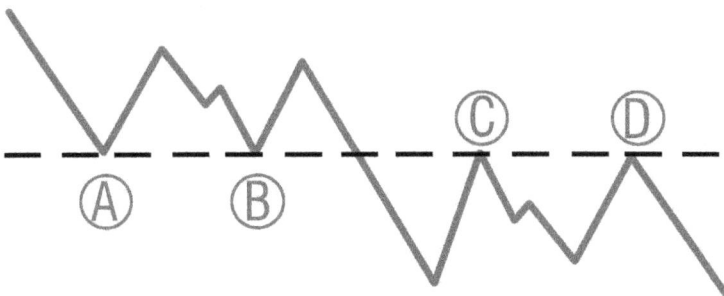

In one of the most basic technical patterns, support often becomes resistance. In the above example, in the time between point B and C, the value of the stock *broke support*. This means that the stock's price dropped past the previous price support levels of A and B. This means that something happened during that timeframe that caused investors to no longer buy or to stop selling shares even at the historic support level. In many cases, after this happens there is a reversal. The former support level will then become resistance. When investors buy again and drive the price back up, it will often have a hard time passing the previous support level and will therefore form a new resistance level right around that price. In this example it is point C and again at point D.

Resistance Becomes Support

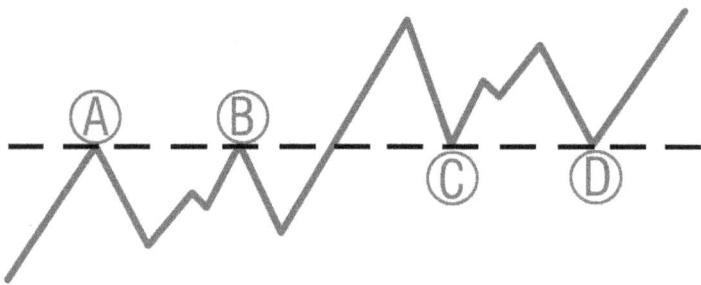

The sample stock chart above shows that the opposite is also true many times. Points A and B are resistance levels, meaning that was the price level which investors deemed was too expensive for that asset. If something causes price levels to go above previous resistance levels, we have what is known as a *technical breakout.* After the breakout, if the price starts to correct and come back down, in many cases the previous resistance levels will become a new support level such as points C and D. Again, the more often you see the support level in the past, the more valid and reliable it is. As a savvy trader, if I was looking at a stock chart and the price is floating around point D, then there is a high probability that the stock will go up from that point. This is because looking back at its price history, I can see that points A and B were former resistance. The stock broke out past that level, then came back to the same price level as support, which is point C. By identifying these factors, I may want to buy the stock at point D, or in other words, *go long* on the stock.

However, If I'm looking at the stock chart in real time and the current price level is somewhere around point B, then there is a high probability that the price will go down. This is because point A has acted as resistance in the past and point B is near that price level. If this were the case in real time, I would *go short* on the stock. In other words I will bet against it because I know there is a high probability that the stock price will go down from there.

How To Short A Stock

Most buy-and-hold investors do not get to profit from downturns in a stock or the market as a whole. Sadly, they miss out on these profit opportunities. As a trader, you can position yourself to make profits during these inevitable times. When you short a stock, you are basically borrowing shares from your broker and immediately selling those shares on the market at the current price. You will later have to return those shares to the broker. In the ideal situation, the stock price would fall so when you buy back those shares to return to the broker, you would pay less than the amount you received when you first borrowed and sold them. Buying shares on the market to return to the broker is called *buying to close*. This overview is exactly what goes on during a short sale situation, and don't worry if it sounds confusing or complex. In real life application all of this is done with a few clicks of your mouse in your trading screen. To summarize, you are basically betting that the price when you close the position will be lower than when you opened it. That price difference, minus fees and commissions, is your profit.

Trend Lines

A trend line is when you use your trading software to literally connect the dots so you can smooth out the picture that the chart is showing you in order to see the overall trend. In the earlier example charts, I used a basic line graph to show the examples more clearly. In real life application you would want to use candlestick charts like this one because they give you more information. You will often draw a trend line between the points of support and the points of resistance. This gives you a general idea of the direction the asset is heading in overall. Support and resistance levels are not always in straight lines. Many times prices move in channels going diagonally up or down. Many traders will consider buying at the support levels and selling when the price nears resistance. On the flip side, resistance levels can give us an idea of when the stock is due for a decline. We can then consider shorting the stock and then closing the position once it nears areas of support again.

Generally, the more times that the support and resistance levels have followed the trend line, the higher the probability that it will continue doing so going forward. Personally, I have to see a price level meet support or resistance at least two to three times in the past on a longer term chart in order to consider it valid going forward. Identifying support and resistance is a fundamental skill of technical analysis. While it is not perfect and 100% accurate, it gives you a higher probability of generating a profitable trade. In investing, high probability and a good risk to reward ratio is all we can ask for.

Flag Patterns

In the sample chart on the next page, we have what is one of the most reliable *continuation patterns*. These are patterns that show merely a pause in the overall trend that is likely to continue after it resolves itself.

FLAG PATTERN

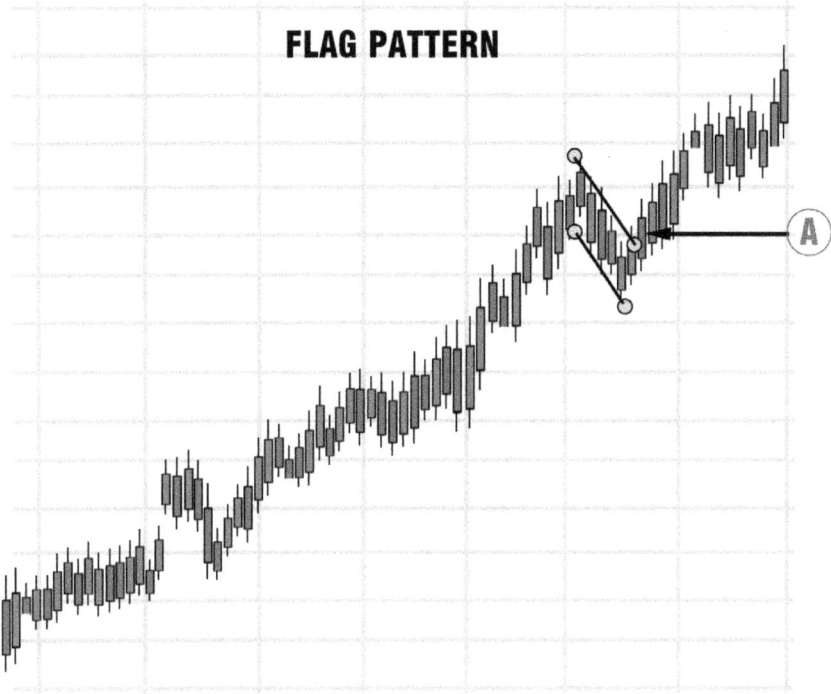

The example above is called a flag pattern simply because when you draw the trend lines, it looks like a flag. The pattern would look like a channel in the opposite direction of the initial upward move. It would create support and resistance levels within that channel. If the price of the asset reaches point A, where a breakout of the upper resistance line occurs, then the pattern holds and there is a high probability that the stock will continue to go up in price.

Triangle Pattern

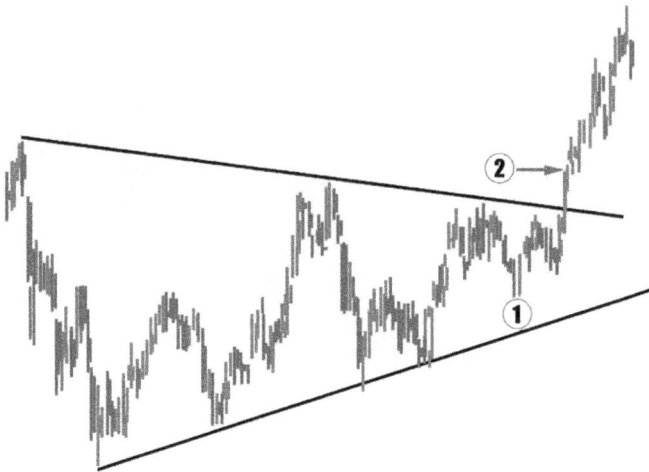

Above is another continuation pattern known as a triangle. It is similar to a flag pattern but the top and bottom trend lines are much steeper, forming a triangle shape. The pattern must start forming soon after a sharp initial upward price move. Most will occur within a few weeks of the sharp initial move. If I see something like this, particularly if the price of the asset goes up above the top resistance line about 2/3rds of the way through the triangle, I know that the stock has a high probability of going up in price. Now you may think, why not buy at the bottom where the price is meeting the bottom of the trend line at point 1 instead of buying at point 2? That trade would make more money right? While that is true, patterns and technical analysis in general is no guarantee — in fact, they are far from it. This is especially true when you're looking at it in real time. It's easy to see a triangle pattern now, but if point 1 was just this morning, it could have broken down past the bottom line, rendering the pattern invalid. So what I would do on the particular stock above is wait until point 2. When the price begins to go in the direction you expect based on a technical pattern, followed by strong volume levels (amount of buyers), then you have what is known as *confirmation*. I never put on a trade unless I have confirmation. It may be a less profitable trade, but it is a high probability one and I prefer to profit less than to lose money.

Head and Shoulders

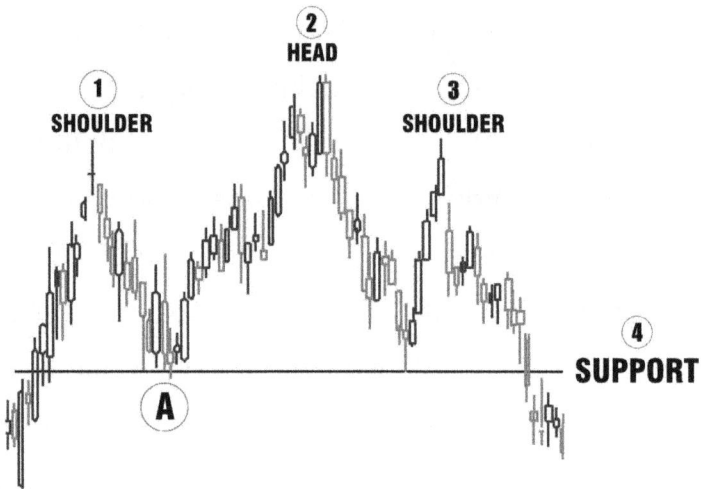

Flag patterns and triangles are continuation patterns, meaning that the trend likely continues after the pattern. Now let's talk about some reliable *reversal patterns*. These are patterns that oftentimes show themselves right before the trend reverses. The head and shoulders is one of the most popular and reliable reversal patterns. In the sample chart above, this stock reached a peak at point 1 then declined all the way back to the support level A. It then broke out past the previous high and made its way all the up to point 2. The uptrend appeared to be intact. However, the stock pulled back all the way to the support level again, also known as the neckline in a head and shoulders pattern. On the following run-up, the price failed to reach or surpass the previous high, point 2. It stopped at point 3 and it began to decline yet again. Point 3 formed the second "shoulder". Shorting a stock a little after point 3 is higher risk / higher profit trade, but full on confirmation only occurs after the stock price breaks down past the neckline (point 4), which was previous support. What this pattern shows you is the psychology of the market. Buyers were trying to push the price higher and they failed to do so at point 3. Those people then gave up on the hope of newer highs and they decide to cash out. Once the neckline support is broken, all faith has been lost in the uptrend of the stock and you have a full-on reversal to the downside.

The patterns that I went over are often reliable when reversed as well. For instance on a down-trending stock you can see a reverse flag or triangle, resulting in the continuation of the downtrend. A reverse head and shoulders occurs when the picture above is flipped upside down where the last "shoulder" fails to reach the lowest low also known as the "head" and then it starts a new uptrend in stock prices. There are numerous patterns out there, some more reliable than others. The ones I present are the some of the most basic and most relied on patterns. They are my go-to patterns for technical analysis of all stocks and funds I have on my watch list.

Fundamental Analysis

While technical analysis involves mainly looking at charts, a fundamental analysis involves looking at financial statements. In the past, generally long term buy-and-hold investors would conduct a fundamental analysis on a company to determine if its price is overvalued or undervalued. Short-term traders would rely more on technical analysis. They were considered the opposite of one another and many who believed in one methodology were often critical and dismissive of the other. The fundamental analyst would argue that the company's financial statement would tell you what the stock price should be worth and will eventually be worth, so no need to look at charts. The technical analyst would say why bother looking at financial statements when the market is already telling us what the stock is worth. It's like the chicken or the egg dilemma.

In recent times it seems that both sides have started coming closer together. Technical analysis has started to gain some mainstream acceptance due to the fact that it just works. To me, it's simple. I'd rather have too much information and signals than not enough. I certainly look at both the fundamentals and the technicals, especially in larger trades. Imagine you're driving to somewhere in your home city but you've never been there before. You know the general area but you would likely have your GPS on too. Relying on only one method of analysis is like relying only on the GPS only and not your eyes. It's like if the GPS tells you to turn left, you see that the road is closed for construction yet you ram your car into the cones anyway. Then on the flip side if you insist on not using your GPS and only using your eyes, you could be driving around for hours wasting time and gas. More information is better than not enough.

A fundamental analysis focuses on the company's financial statement. There you can get an overview of the company's health. You will see revenues and expenses as well as assets and liabilities. By looking at revenues and expenses you can see if a company is profitable or if it is losing money. It's a snapshot of the company's performance in the short term. By looking at assets and liability you can see how much debt the company has. If you're looking at a scenario where expenses are higher than income, and liabilities are more than assets, you can come to the logical conclusion that the company can't make money even by leveraging itself. Chances are it will have a hard time paying back that debt since it isn't even profitable. You might not want to invest in that stock no matter what the charts tell you. On the other hand, if the company makes healthy profits and its liabilities are relatively low, then you can feel more comfortable going long on the stock.

For the fundamental analyst, stock prices don't necessary reflect the quality of the company you are looking to invest in. The stock price doesn't really matter. You can't expect a $200 stock to be somehow better than a $100 stock. In order to find the true value of the stock, we use key figures that are universally applied to all stocks so we can compare one company to a similar one.

Price/Earnings (PE Ratio)

PE Ratio = Market value per share ÷ Earnings per Share

If company A's stock is $20 per share and its earnings were $1.25 per share, you would have a PE ratio of 16. A trailing P/E takes the earnings per share (EPS) from the past four quarters while the forward P/E uses earnings estimates on what the next four quarters would be. The higher the PE ratio, the more money investors are willing to pay for a certain level of earnings. Therefore, in theory, the lower the PE ratio, the "cheaper" the stock is when you are comparing two similar stocks.

So company A has a PE ratio of 16. What does this tell us? By itself it doesn't tell us much other than fact that the company is profitable since companies that lose money won't have a PE ratio reported because they don't have earnings. To get a better sense of the value of this company's stock, we can compare it to another company that is similar. That could mean a company in the same industry and of similar size. In the previous example, company A's stock was $20 per share with an earnings per share of $1.75. We can then compare it to a similar company, let's call it B, whose stock price is $40 per share with a earnings per share of $2.75. 40 divided by 2.75 would give us a PE ratio of 14.5. On paper, the lower the PE ratio, the better the deal you are getting. It means you are paying less for earnings with company B even though the stock price is $40 and company A's stock price is $20. At the time of calculation, company B appears to be the better bargain. You are paying less per share for a certain level of earnings.

Price/Earnings to Growth (PEG ratio)

PEG ratio = PE Ratio ÷ Annual EPS Growth

Sometimes a PE ratio doesn't tell us the whole picture. It tells us the price we are paying for earnings at a given time, but it doesn't tell us much about the future. Some investors will pay extraordinarily high PE ratios in anticipation of future earnings. The earnings growth rate tells you about the momentum of the company in addition to the current snapshot. Let's take a look the previous examples again. We determined that company B, with a PE ratio of 14.5 looked more attractive than company A, which had a PE ratio of 16. 16 seems more expensive. But what if company A had a growth rate of 10% while company B had a growth rate of only 6%? In this case, company A would have a PEG of 1.6 (16 divided by 10) and company B would have a PEG of 2.42 (14.5 divided by 6). As it would turn out, company A has more growth momentum, and thus would be a better bargain in the long run.

These ratios, among others, are used to determine the performance of a company in relation to its stock price.

The primary benefit is to use it as a benchmark to compare to similar companies. This is like looking at compareables on a house or car before you purchase one. Fundamental analysis also takes into account outside factors such as the economy as a whole. These are external factors that can affect the overall stock market, such as unemployment rate, inflation, consumer spending, national debt, personal debt, interest rates, military conflicts and even terrorism.

Essentially, there are certain things that can happen that will cause a market-wide sell off or a run-up that doesn't make sense when looking at the charts or even the company's performance. At the time of this writing, the overall stock market is having a hard time figuring out the direction it wants to go in. Concerns about interest rates and even foreign (Greek) debt is causing unusual movements in the markets. When going long or short on a stock, a smart investor would pay attention to the state of the economy as a whole. Remember, the more information you have the better.

Stock Trading Strategies For Success

Like anything in life, nothing worth having comes easy. Successful investing is a skill. Developing that skill takes dedication and practice over a long period of time. It is that willingness to put in effort that separates profitable investors from everyone else who is essentially gambling. I have utilized certain strategies that have helped me acclimate to the world of stocks with minimized risk and efficient learning processes. They are included in this section.

Learn for Free

Open an online brokerage account. You can decide which one you want to go with. I have several accounts for different purposes, but I primarily use TD Ameritrade because I like their Think or Swim trading software. It is amazing, professional-grade software and it's 100% free. Once you open the account, go to their education section and spend a weekend going through everything there. There are excellent free resources provided by your broker including videos, guides and sometimes even seminars. Your broker has a vested interest in your success so they will spend the money to produce high quality educational tools. When I first got into trading I spent a week straight reading and watching all the free material provided by both TD Ameritrade and Etrade. Although a lot of the things may be repetitive, it is still worth reviewing.

After opening an account, you can download the trading software that your broker provides usually for free. In my case it is Think or Swim (TOS) by TD Ameritrade. Most of these platforms offer a paper-trading mode. You sign up and boom, you get $100,000 (or another large amount) in fake money to trade with. You can practice the different principles and go through actual real life trades without risking a dime. It also allows you to get used to the software itself as these platforms are a bit complex and overwhelming in the beginning. Paper trading is 100% the same as real life trading. It is the exact same experience but with "fake" money. It is best to paper trade for 6 months to a year. Patience will definitely pay off in this case.

Technical Analysis

You must study and master technical analysis. I suggest picking up books where the subject is just on technical analysis alone. Read reviews, go for timeless titles, nothing trendy. Avoid anything that promises a special trading technique or something that promises huge returns. Look for textbook style material on technical analysis. My favorite is Technical Analysis of the Financial Markets by John Murphy.

Easy Fundamentals

When it comes to fundamental analysis, we can look up balance sheets and calculate PE and PEG ratios for companies all day, but that is not an efficient use of our time. Lucky for us, information is abundant these days. Most of the homework has been done for you. Financial websites like Yahoo Finance or your own broker such as Etrade will have the fundamentals listed. The ratios will be there, the financials statements available, and most importantly they usually include simplified links to multiple analyses conducted by people who do it for a living. Usually you'll see a breakdown showing a buy, hold, or sell recommendation or a number or star scale showing the overall recommendation of the analyst. These recommendations are usually made by taking into account all the important fundamental factors compared against similar companies. I leverage the expertise of these professionals who do fundamental analysis for a living and develop an overall consensus. I'll use Yahoo Finance coupled with multiple analyst recommendations from Etrade and get a holistic average of what these people are saying about the company. If I take a significant long position, even for a short term, I would make sure that there are a good amount of "buy" recommendations in addition to the stock chart itself. To be more specific, I would use the fundamental analysis to determine if I should even get in to begin with, and use technical analysis to determine at which point exactly would I want to get in and get out for maximum profit.

Small Positions

The best way to ease yourself into successful trading is to start with small positions, meaning buying or shorting less shares. Being successful as a trader involves skill sets such as technical and fundamental analysis, but it also means controlling your emotions so you can make better decisions. It takes extreme discipline to do what is right in the face of emotional reactions. Undisciplined people make the wrong investment choices. Think about it. What do people do when the stock or real estate market goes up to new highs? They often keep buying or hold on to their positions because they think it'll go up forever. They are overcome with confidence, so they unknowingly put themselves at risk. The same goes for the down side. When things are collapsing all around you, the emotional reaction would be to bail. Once people start to sell everyone starts to sell and the feeling is that things will keep getting worse. Most people reacting on emotion will not buy during these worst of times. It is only those who are disciplined and keep their emotions in check who will pick up the bargains. Warren Buffett once said perhaps the wisest words for investing: "be fearful when others are greedy and greedy when others are fearful".

Even after paper trading, you want to set yourself up mentally and emotionally for live trades. When I decided to take investing seriously, I started very small, buying few shares. I either made a bit of money or lost a bit of money. It wasn't sexy or exciting, but it wasn't meant to be. This process is designed to test your hypothesis while keeping your emotions in check. With such small risk and reward, you won't let the emotions of greed or fear dictate your decisions to buy or sell. As your confidence grows and you become accustomed to taking wins and some losses, then you slowly get into larger positions and everything will come naturally.

Cutting Losses

Learning to cut losses is a skill in itself. It also has to do with controlling your emotions. Even with all of our tools, resources and information, sometimes the stock price will just go against you. The amazing thing about a lot of successful traders is the fact that they aren't even right most of the time. As a matter of fact you can make a ton of money even if you're wrong more than half the time. The key is to cut losses quickly when you are wrong. It requires a lot of discipline because the natural and emotional reaction to approaching a trade that goes against you is to hold and see if it comes back. For example if a stock heads down towards a support area, you may buy thinking it's going to go up from there. If the price goes down instead and breaks that support line, emotional investors will hold on thinking it will surely come back. However, if you were a rational person just coming into the trade, seeing that the price has broken support, you may even be tempted to short the stock. Shorting the stock at that time would be a better trade but you won't see that because you are in the trade with a long position and emotions are keeping you from selling and taking the small loss.

Disciplined traders have a mental stop-loss point before they even get into the position. They set up risk versus reward scenarios. They determine how much would they be willing to risk if they are wrong in exchange for the greater reward if they are right. If the stock price goes against them and hits the mental stop loss price level, the disciplined trader will cut losses and get out immediately. The big takeaway is that for the disciplined trader, even if they are wrong more times than they are right, they will still be profitable overall because the profits made when they are right covers the small losses taken when they are wrong.

Find Mentors and Advisors

When it comes to both business and investing, mentors and advisors will help you achieve your goals faster and more efficiently. The most successful people from billionaires to the president have advisors. By leveraging the expertise and knowledge of others, you are saving both time and unnecessary setbacks. When it comes to investing, I have a team of trusted mentors and advisors that I hear from daily. I receive different perspectives on the economy, the markets, and global concerns. In the past, this exchange of information would be done in actual face-to-face meetings or video conferencing. That type of arrangement is expensive, which is why usually only the wealthy had advisors. Nowadays with the internet, your team of advisors communicate with you in newsletters, blog posts and sometimes video.

For an introduction to my personal team of advisors, sign up for the most current version of this stock investing course on my blog SevenFigureLife.com. It is a free email course that contains the most up to date lessons in addition to an intro to my personal advisors, all of whom are self-made millionaire investors themselves.

Intro To Options

Trading stocks is relatively straightforward. You usually buy and sell them when you believe prices are going up, or you short sell then cover if you believe that prices are going down. Adding option strategies to your tool belt gives you an added dimension of trading. Sophisticated investors have been utilizing options for decades. Options can help you generate higher profits and reduce potential losses. The three primary benefits of options are leverage, hedging and income. You can use options to control a large amount of stocks for a fraction of what it would cost to own those shares. You can also use options as an insurance policy for shares you already own. Lastly, options allow you to generate an additional income from shares that you own and even shares that you don't even own.

What is an option?

An option is a contract that gives the buyer the right, but not the obligation to buy or sell an asset (usually a stock or an index fund) at a specific price on or before a certain expiration date. To better explain this concept, imagine someone is selling a house for $275,000. I want to buy it because I have knowledge that the area is going to be re-zoned from a poorly ranked school district to a very good school district in the coming months, which will make the house worth about $350,000. However, it's not finalized and no announcement was made by the planning committee. I don't want to pay full price for the house after the re-zoning is announced and I don't want to buy the house and be stuck with it if the school deal never happens. To solve my dilemma, I negotiate an option contract with the seller and tell him I'll give him $3000 for the right to buy the house for $300,000 and the option would be good for 2 months. The seller has nothing to lose because I'm offering a price higher than asking and if I don't buy it, he gets to keep the $3000 and sell the house to someone else anyway. If the school deal goes through, I can exercise my right to buy the house at $300,000. If I choose to exercise that option, I would pay $303,000 for a home that will then be worth $350,000. The difference, minus fees is my profit. If the school deal does not happen, I lose $3000 and simply let the option expire. I never buy the house.

In this example, the $3000 figure would be the *premium*, which is the price of the option. The $300,000 figure is the *strike price*, which is the price that I have the right, but not the obligation to buy the asset at. Two months from the day I buy the option is the *expiration*, after which the option is completely worthless. This is a general idea of how options work. This scenario is beneficial to me as a buyer because I stand to profit from the deal by only putting up $3,000 rather than $300,000. The seller benefits by generating an additional $3,000 income from his asset with the possibility of selling it at a higher price.

Now let's move on to the application in the stock market. In a hypothetical example, let's say you think ABC computer company (a fictitious stock) is going to rebound from the reliable support level it's currently at, which is $120. You think the stock price will move towards $130 in the coming weeks or months. The stock is not cheap, so if you want 100 shares of ABC, you have to have $12,000 + commissions in your brokerage account. For a lot of people in Phase 2 of the wealth building journey, that can be a significant portion of the account. Another way is to buy a *call option* on ABC computer company. Option contracts are usually priced per 100 shares. Let's say that the option costs $2/share for the

$125 strike price that expires in 2 months. That $2 price is multiplied by 100 shares, meaning the option contract will cost you $200. That is the premium that you would pay in this example.

ABC computer company

Current Stock Price = $120

Option Price at $125 Strike Price = $2 per share

1 Option Contract = 100 shares

Premium = $200 per contract

If ABC's stock price moves in the favor of your trade, and it reaches $130 before your expiration date, you can exercise your option and buy the 100 shares for $125 a share. If that were the case you would have paid $12,700 (($125 X 100) + $200 option premium) for 100 shares of stock that is currently worth $13,000 ($130 X 100). If you sell your shares immediately, you have a profit of $300 minus fees. If you bought 2 option contracts for $400 premium instead of 1, your profit would be $600 minus fees. If you bought 10 option contracts when the stock was at $120, you would have a $3000 profit minus fees.

There are two main benefits of buying option contracts rather than just buying the stock outright. For one, you are using leverage. For only $200 you are controlling those 100 shares instead of tying up $12,000 needed to buy those 100 shares outright at the $120 price. In this scenario, your $200 investment for the premium made a $300 profit. That gives you a return on investment (ROI) of 50% ignoring fees and commissions. If you bought the shares for $12,000 and sold at $13,000, your profit is $1000. However, since you had to risk a significantly higher amount of money, your return on investment is less than 10%. Leverage helps you reduce your upfront investment and increase your ROI. As mentioned in the beginning of this chapter, the second benefit of options is hedging and limited risk. In this example, if you purchase the option for $200, that caps your risk at that amount. Even in the worst-case scenario, you would have only lost the $200 premium that you paid. Even if the stock falls to $0 you only lose that $200. If you bought the 100 shares for $12,000 and the stock goes against you from the moment you purchase, you can lose a lot more money.

There are 2 types of options contracts, known as calls and puts. A *call option* is a contract like the previous example where you have the right to buy a certain number of stocks at a certain price within a certain amount of time. You are generally hoping that the stock will go up past your strike price before expiration. The second type of options contract is called a put. A *put option* is the opposite of a call. It gives the buyer of the contract the right but not the obligation to sell shares at a certain price before expiration. This means you want the stock price to go down below your strike price. In many cases, if you think a stock will go up, you buy a call option. If you think it will go down, you'll buy a put option.

Selling Options

The great thing about options is that you don't have to be just on the buying side. You can sell options to the market as well. When you are a seller of options, you are known as the *option writer.* This is a great way to generate income using options. Lets take a look at the ABC computer example again.

ABC computer company

Current Stock Price = $120

Option Price at $125 Strike = $2 per share

Premium = $200

In the previous example, you are looking to buy an options contract because you think that the stock is going from $120 to $130. Me, I'm looking at the charts and reading about future products, and I feel that their glory days are behind them and there's no way it's going to hit $130 or even past $125. So I'm on the other end and I choose to sell an options contract at the $125 strike price to the market. In that case, I would receive that $200 premium upfront. If I'm right, and the stock stays under $125, the option expires and I get an easy $200. If you're right and you decided to exercise the option when the stock is $130, then I am obligated to buy 100 shares at current market price and give you those shares, while you only have to pay me $125 a share. I would lose $500 plus fees and commissions, but I do get to keep that $200 premium either way. Being able to sell options opens the door to many income generation possibilities.

Options are a Derivative

An interesting thing about options is that a lot of traders buy and sell options with no intention of ever exercising that right to buy or sell the stock. They simply use it simply as a form of leverage so they don't have to actually buy shares of stock. The reason is because options are a derivative, which basically means that they are assets with a value that is based on the value of something else, usually the underlying stock or the index. Because of that, you can buy and sell options before the expiration date.

Example:

ABC computer company

Current Stock Price = $120

Option Price at $125 Strike = $2 per 100 share Contract

Premium = $200

ABC computer company (3 weeks later)

Current Stock Price = $124

Option Price at $125 Strike = $4 per 100 share Contract

Premium = $400

In the previous ABC computer company example, let's say you bought the options contract with the strike price of $125 when the stock was at $120 because you believed it was going to go up to $130. Within three weeks, the stock price jumps up to $124. However, it's showing signs of weakness, there's some bad press and you no longer think it'll hit the $130 price target. At this point, you can choose to close your position (sell your options contract) right then and there and take a profit. It wouldn't make sense to exercise the option and buy the stock at $125 a share because that's more expensive than the $124 market price. Because you bought your option when ABC was at $120, you paid a relatively low price for that option. Now your contract is worth more to someone else because ABC is at $124, which is just $1 less than your $125 strike price. For someone who still thinks ABC will hit $130 or more, they would be willing to pay more than the $2/share ($200 contract) you paid. They would now have to pay $4/share ($400 contract) because the odds are higher than the contract will be profitable. In this example, if you sell your options contract, you would have received $400 for something that you paid $200 for, making you a sweet 100% return on investment. You made money on your call options contract because the price of the underlying stock went up. As you can see, when you trade options, you are essentially experiencing the same effect as buying the shares without putting up as much money.

Gamblers in the Options Market

Options are extremely versatile financial instruments. They allow you to be more adaptive to different market conditions. It opens up a completely new dimension of trading. However, that being said, options come with added risk too. Unsophisticated investors abuse options and basically use them for high-risk speculation. Say for instance on the ABC computer company example where the stock is trading at $120, gamblers would go and buy 10 call options on ABC computer company with a strike price of $140, expiring in 2 months. They'll do something like that because it's "cheap", maybe something like $20 per contract in this hypothetical example. These far-out options contracts are cheap because no one thinks the stock price will increase drastically like that in just 2 months. It sounds inexpensive, with a nice payday if they are right, but in most cases they will be wrong and they will just lose $200. ($20 per contract x 10 contracts).

Blind speculation is gambling and gambling is not investing. Consider this. If you have $20,000 in your brokerage account and lose 20% over a series of risky "home run" trades, that leaves you with $16,000. Just to get your account back to break even ($20,000), you now need a 25% gain ($4000 return on $16,000). Taking big risks, losing money and then taking even bigger risks to try to make up for it is the worst downward cycle amateur traders and gamblers can get themselves into.

Options Strategies for Success

When used properly, options can increase your ROI with less upfront risk. They can be an income generator and even act as an insurance policy. In this section I'll share with you some options strategies that I use that involve limited risk, so you don't put yourself into the gambler category and blow up your account. That's something to avoid at all costs. Consistent gains are better than big risks that set you back big time. Some strategies that I talk about involve being in multiple positions during the duration of the trade. These types of strategies are called options spreads. A spread is when you buy and sell multiple options contracts as one overall position. Here are some of the best options strategies used by beginners as well as seasoned veterans.

Cash Secured Put

A cash-secured put is an income strategy that allows you to potentially buy shares at a discounted price. This strategy lets you get paid while you wait for the price to get a bit cheaper. If you are bullish on a stock, but the stock is not exactly trading at the price you want to buy it at, you could sell a put option at the strike price where you would be comfortable buying the 100 shares at. You would be required to have enough money in your account to buy those shares if necessary. Say a stock is trading at $24 a share and you think it will to go up in the near future. However, you are still more comfortable buying it at $20. You would sell a put option at the strike price of $20. Remember, when you sell (write) an options contract, you get paid that premium. So in this case you would get paid upfront for that put option that you've sold. If the stock hits that $20 level or slightly below it, the buyer of that option may exercise it because he was betting it would go down. This means you have to buy those the stock at $20 per share. That was what you wanted anyway because you would be paying that $20 per share instead of $24 and you still keep the premium from the put option you have sold. If the stock price never drops down to $20 by the expiration of the option you sold, then it simply expires and you keep the premium. With this strategy you get paid over and over, while waiting for that stock to go on sale.

Another way utilize the cash-secured put strategy is to aim only for low risk income. I sell puts all the time with no intention on ever buying the shares. I aim to make around $500 - $1000 in a few weeks on each of these types of trades. It's a safe income strategy for me. I monitor a group of stocks or indexes and sell puts below the historic support levels. If you remember what support is from the technical analysis chapter, it is a price level where the stock is expected to rebound because it has done so many times in the past. In the previous example, the stock is at $24 and looks to be on an uptrend. Sophisticated traders may want to get in at the support level of $20, so they'll use cash-secured puts to generate good income while they wait. If this is one of my low-risk income plays, I'll sell the put options at the $18 strike price rather than at the $20 level because I have no intention of buying the shares whatsoever. I just want the income. The premium I would get would be lower than at the $20 strike price, but the probability that I would ever have to buy the shares is lower. While I generally want just the income from the premium alone in these cases, I'll gladly buy the shares if I am forced to. I know that at the $18 bargain price, I'll likely make money when the price goes up in addition to the premium that I was already paid. To me, that would be a win-win trade.

Covered Calls

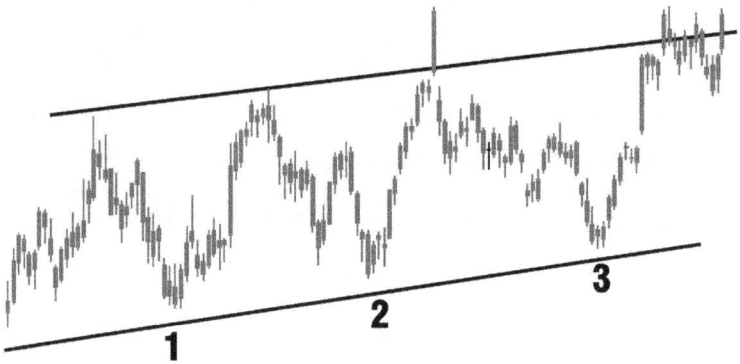

If I see a chart of a stock and it looks something like the one above, I'm running covered calls on that asset all day. This strategy is used when you already own shares of a stock, but you want to extract more money out of it in the form of premium income. Let's say you used the cash-secured put in the previous example to buy 100 shares of a stock at that $20 discounted price. Now you own those shares and you believe it's headed towards $30. You can go ahead and sell a call option against those shares that you own. You can sell a call option at a strike price where you wouldn't mind selling your shares at. The further away the strike price is from the current price of the stock, the less premium you will get. Say you sell a call option at the $25 strike price. That gives you a good premium and you won't mind giving up your shares at that price. First you keep that premium, that money is yours. Now if the stock goes up and passes $25, you'll likely be *called*, meaning the buyer exercises his option and you must sell him your shares at $25 per share. In this example, you made $5 per share ($500 profit) and you keep the premium for the option contract that you sold as well. Now if the stock does not reach or pass $25 by the expiration of the option contract, then it makes no sense for the buyer to exercise the option. The option will likely just expire and you simply keep the premium (income) you were paid for selling the option contract.

This strategy is also known as a synthetic dividend. If you plan to own shares of a stock or fund for a longer period, you can repeatedly sell call options to generate passive income. You would generally sell those call options at strike prices higher than what you think the stock price will be at prior to expiration. The purpose is to generate income with no intention of selling your shares. For example, at any given time I will hold shares of an ETF that tracks the price of silver (symbol SLV). I'm bullish on silver in the long run, especially at the prices I pay. What I will do is sell call options around 1 month out at strike prices that are well above what I think the price will go to in a month. I have no intention of selling my shares. I just want income. This strategy allows me to collect options premiums every single month like rent, while I wait for my shares to appreciate over time. If on any given month the price of silver shoots up and reaches the strike price of the options I have sold, then I will be forced to sell my shares. However, I would make money from the appreciation of my shares as well as the premium that I was paid. It is a win - win either way. If that happened, I just have to run the cash secured put strategy mentioned earlier on symbol SLV and collect premiums that way until I buy my shares back at a discounted price. In nearly all outcomes I would be generating profits and income.

Collar

A collar is sort of like the combination of the two strategies I just mentioned. You own shares of a stock or fund that you think will go up in value. You sell call options against the number of shares that you own. For example if you bought 100 shares then you can sell 1 call option against it. If you own 200 shares you can sell 2 call options, etc. You would sell at a strike price above what you paid for the stock, and at the same time you buy a put option below what you paid for the stock. Because you're in 2 positions at the same time, this strategy is called an options spread.

The put option that you buy acts as insurance and caps your loss in case the stock unexpectedly turns against you or if there is a significant sell-off event in the market in general. Imagine buying a stock where you can still experience the upside profits but your risk and loss is capped at a minimal amount even if the stock loses 20%, 50% or 90% of its value. In addition to that, the premium that you get from selling the call option often times pays for most, if not all of the put option that you buy. In the world of stocks, this is as close to free insurance as you can get.

Long Call Spread

The long call spread, aka bull call spread, aka vertical spread is a bullish options strategy. With this strategy, you believe a stock will go up in value in the short term, but you do not own the stock. Maybe it's a $50, $100, or even $300 stock and you don't want to put in that kind of money into a position and buy the stock outright so you utilize call options. Here you are buying call options at a strike price that is right at or very close to the current price of the stock, known as an *at the money* option. At the same time you would be selling the same number of contracts, at the same expiration above the current stock price. For example if the stock in question is $30 per share, you would buy a call option at the $30 strike price and sell a call option at the $35 strike price. If the stock jumps to $38 per share, you are forced to provide 100 shares to the buyer of that $35 call option. Since you don't own the shares, you would exercise the call option that you purchased at the $30 strike price. With that call option you have the right to buy the 100 shares at $30. You would exercise your option to buy at $30 per share and sell to the other option buyer for $35 per share. Your profit is $5 per share minus fees and commissions. In this example, you were able to control 100 shares of a $30 stock then sell those 100 shares for $35 per share without having to actually purchase 100 shares for $3,000 to begin with.

This strategy beats simply buying the $30 strike call option alone because the premium that you collect by selling the $35 strike price call option will help to offset the cost of the option you bought. This limits your risk to only what you paid for the option after selling one as well. You can be completely wrong about the stock and it tanks in value, but you only lose what you paid for the option. The traditional way of going long on a stock you are bullish about is to buy the shares outright. When you buy shares outright, you have to invest a significantly higher amount of money, and you are not protected against big losses.

Long Put Spread

The long put spread is simply the opposite of the long call spread. You utilize this strategy when you think a stock is overbought or near its long-term resistance area, which is the price level that historically the stock had a hard time surpassing. In short, you think the price is coming down. You do not own the stock in this case, nor are you shorting the stock. This strategy involves selling a put which is around the target area of where you think the stock price will fall to. For example if a stock is at $40, and you think it will drop to $35 or lower in the coming weeks, you would sell a put option at the $35 strike price and at the same time buy a put option at $40. Both options will have the same expiration. If the price of the asset drops from $40 to $32, you would exercise your option to sell the shares at $40 and purchase at $35. You would make $5 per share in this case, minus fees and commissions.

With this strategy, the sale of the lower strike put option helps to offset some of the cost of buying the *at the money* put option. Your total risk is only the net amount you paid for the put option after selling one as well. This strategy beats simply shorting the stock because your risk is capped at the price you paid for the put option. When you short the stock, you borrow the shares from your broker to sell to the market, hoping to be buying later at a cheaper price. If you are completely wrong and the stock goes up in value, you stand to lose a large amount of money when you return those shares. In a long put spread, you only lose the options premium cost that you paid.

Long Straddle

The long straddle is a very simple setup that does not involve owning actual shares of stock. You buy a call and you buy a put simultaneously at the exact same strike price. What this means is that you believe that there is going to be a big move in the price of the stock or fund you're tracking. Maybe your analysis shows that the stock or fund is in the dead center of a big trading range on the chart and it never stays in that area for long historically. Or the company has a major deal pending but is not yet finalized. You know the stock price is either going way up or way down based on that. You don't know which direction it will go, nor do you care. You just know it's not staying at the price it is now. With this strategy, the underlying asset has to make a big move in either direction. If it goes up or down but the move isn't big enough, you can still lose money. However, your maximum risk is limited to what you paid for both that call and that put. So far I haven't come across many situations where I had to use this strategy. But it is always a tool in your belt when you're dealing with volatile times in the market as a whole or a company going through a major shakeup. Once in a while these things happen, such the Federal Reserve announcing an interest rate change, or a failing company that is in merger talks.

Iron Condor

The iron condor is a pure income strategy that involves 4 options contracts. The idea is to identify stocks, index funds or commodity funds that are trading fairly reliably within a range, meaning it tends to move sort of sideways and doesn't tend to break out above a certain price level or break down below a certain price level in the course of one or two months. Your goal is for the stock's price to stay in between two specific price areas. Remember, stocks will often move in channels so this strategy can be used in many market conditions, not just sideways price movements alone. We can use iron condors in an uptrend or a downtrend. Iron condors are more profitable during times of high volatility when options contracts generally cost more.

Here in this chart, you see that within a year, this stock tends to trade between $30 and $40 and you believe that trend will continue so you want to deploy the iron condor strategy. You would sell a put at the the $30 strike price as well as sell a call at the $40 level. However, you would want some protection in case the stock decides to break out or break down past those levels for whatever reason. So to protect yourself you will also buy a put at a strike price below the low range and buy a call above the high range. As long as the stock price stays within those levels by expiration, you keep the entire premium that you collected minus what you paid for the protective put and the protective call. If the stock goes above or below your ranges, then your protective put or call will cap your loss. This is a pure income strategy because you are simply collecting premiums and making sure that your underlying stock stays within the range that you set your iron condor at. Your risk is also capped. When it comes to these more complex trades involving multiple options contracts, most trading software will show you the maximum gain and maximum loss associated with it before you make the trade.

Tying it all Together

You'll notice that in all these trading strategies and concepts, everything tends to tie together. Technical analysis helps you make high probability predictions of price directions in the short term. By seeing support and resistance levels and recognizing patterns, you're more equipped to make a confident trade. Then, depending on which particular stock or fund you're looking at, what your analysis tells you and other factors, you can buy the stock and run options strategies on that position, or just run the options strategies without buying any shares. As you progress and develop your skills, patterns become easier to identify and knowing which strategy to run is like thinking "hammer" when you see a nail sticking out on your wall.

If you're new to trading, what you just read may be very overwhelming but also enlightening. You likely feel excited, intimidated, or both. That is totally normal. When I first got into trading I knew I wanted to make money but the stuff was so overwhelming with all the terms and the charts. It all seemed pretty crazy. But like anything else, once you become educated and get some practice, things become second nature.

As you recall in the beginning of this book, I mentioned that investing is Phase 2 of wealth building. I don't think you should even look into advanced trading before you maximize your personal income by working on your business. It goes hand in hand. In successful trading, you want to become systematic and cut out all emotion. When you're trading with purely spare money, it's easier to cut out emotion because income keeps coming in and living expenses are covered. Far too many people get ahead of themselves and try to make a killing in stocks before even establishing a stable source of business income. Focus more on building and growing a low risk, high reward business such as an e-commerce store or a blog business. These fundamental strategies will never change and the stock market isn't going anywhere.

The scope of this book is to introduce you to trading and the various tools that are available to you. I want you to get excited and be aware of the possibilities that are ahead of you. What I've mentioned here is just the tip of the iceberg. It is as simplified as possible, but at the same time I understand that a lot of it may still seem complex to a lot of people. It will all make sense, don't worry. I didn't want to get into more complex spreads, how to adjust positions, and the many, many more details about stocks and options trading. Trading is something that takes years to master, but you owe it to yourself and your loved ones to learn and put your future in your own hands rather than relying on the financial services industry. The great thing is, with the lifestyle that an online business provides, you will be in the perfect situation and environment to master the art of trading. All you need is a computer and some time.

Wealth Journey Phase 3: Passive Income

During the first phase of the Seven Figure Life wealth journey, you'll work to build online businesses to generate revenue. As the businesses grow and stabilize, your time and location freedom allows you to move on to the second phase. In Phase 2, you'll position your money to work for you. The business income is re-invested to maximize the velocity of wealth accumulation. In Phase 3, the focus is to generate passive income while preserving that accumulated wealth. The Phase 3 entrepreneur seeks reliable income and secure assets. For generations, the wealthy have turned to one asset class that provides those benefits: real estate.

Stocks vs. Real Estate

Are stocks better, or is real estate better? I hear financial experts argue with each other all the time over which is the superior option, and I can't help but laugh a little because it's never one or the other. Both are timeless and proven investment vehicles. I utilize both, and I look at it like this: learning to trade stocks is a wealth accumulation strategy. Investing in real estate is more of a retirement income plan and a wealth preservation strategy. In other words, stocks are better suited for Phase 2 of the wealth journey and real estate is better suited for Phase 3. Let's go over several reasons why we arrive at this conclusion.

Investable Capital

The first thing to consider is the amount of investable capital you have available. Most Phase 2 entrepreneurs have $10,000, $20,000, maybe even $50,000 of investible capital. This won't even get you in the door in most big cities, but in smaller cities it may be do-able. If you find a property for sale in a decent neighborhood, chances are the cash on cash return on your investment will be well under 10% annually. That is an extremely slow way to grow your wealth. Then you have to maintain the property, keep reserves for repairs, and manage people. To me, it's simply not worth my time to deal with it for such a small return, both percentage-wise and dollar-wise. If you take the time to study strategies and learn how to trade stocks, you can make a lot more money doing a lot less work with an account size of $20,000 - $50,000.

I know there are people who sell books and talk about how you can buy with 0 down by using leverage and other people's money, etc. The bottom line is those types of high leverage scenarios often produce zero or even negative returns. Don't even think about buying a piece of real estate that is cash-flow negative. That's not even in the conversation because that is real estate speculation aka gambling, not real investing. In these cases, what you are doing is creating yourself a new liability. You will be dumping more and more money every month into a black hole and hoping that appreciation bails you out. Appreciation should be looked at as a bonus, not something to rely on. The last time I checked, something that requires that you consistently put in money and hope for a big payout is either called a slot machine or a Nigerian email scam. Most people in either case won't get rich.

Now picture yourself as a Phase 3 entrepreneur looking to invest in real estate. When you get to the point where you have hundreds of thousands of dollars to invest, then the conversation changes. At that point, it is smart to purchase good quality real estate as a form of wealth preservation and to enjoy reliable passive income from rents. Though the cash on cash return on investment may still be low, the dollar amount would be high. You may see a relatively low 6-12% ROI, which is actually typical for good properties in good areas as of this writing.

However, that usually translates to thousands of dollars per month in the form of passive income. That's the difference compared to the Phase 2 entrepreneurs' scenario, where the 6-12% ROI only means a few hundred dollars a month because they are working with less money and smaller deals. When you're talking thousands of dollars a month, then it is worth the time to deal with tenants or simply hire a property manager. It's worth accepting the lower percentage return, too, because you will be reliably collecting a significant-sized check every month.

Liquidity

Lastly, and perhaps the most important reason to hold off on real estate as a Phase 2 entrepreneur is because stocks are liquid and real estate is not. Again, my strategy for anything involves high potential profits while minimizing risk. Too many writers and financial gurus ignore risk management. When you are in wealth accumulation mode, meaning only 5 figures in investable capital, you can spread that into quite a number of trades at any given time in the stock market. In real estate, 5 figures means that just about all of that money will be in only one property at a time with perhaps a bit of reserve funds. Talk about all your eggs in one basket! If you get yourself into a single bad trade on a single stock or fund, you simply cut your losses quickly and get out. This can literally be done in minutes and maybe you'll lose a few hundred dollars. If you get yourself into a bad real estate deal, you can be on the hook for months and the deal can die a slow painful death. In a single bad deal you can lose thousands of dollars, your entire initial investment, or in some cases even more money than you initially put in. Think about this. The commission and fees alone to sell a property is already in the thousands. This is one asset class that is by no means liquid.

When I talk about liquidity risk, I speak from personal experience. I made my first real estate investment when I was in college. I had a real estate license at the time and I put all of my commissions and some business savings into buying a rental house. Long story short, poor ROI combined with unexpected repairs led to a total loss of around $35,000. That was a significant chunk of my investable cash at the time. It's not only a one-time loss either. You have to think long term. That loss happened to me a long time ago and had I been more careful and allocated the funds to liquid investments, those funds would likely be worth well over $100,000 by now even by conservative figures. Over the course of a lifetime, that

$35,000 lost likely translates to a million dollars or more in opportunity cost. That is why liquidity and being able to cut losses quickly is extremely important as a Phase 2 entrepreneur. Unlike a big corporation, you don't have the leisure of a government bailout if you make bad choices and toxic investments.

This costly lesson taught me the difference between investing and speculation, as well as the importance of liquidity. With that experience, I discovered that wealth is built in phases. I needed to be persistent but also be patient. I focused on building my businesses and learning to invest in stocks. After a few years of growing my businesses and starting new ones, I focused on trading. I eventually became consistently profitable in the markets and grew my accounts substantially. Now, I'm in real estate to preserve that accumulated wealth and to build more passive income. My wealth-building journey consisted of building online businesses, allocating a portion to investing in the stock market to accelerate wealth accumulation, then rolling a significantly larger chunk of investable cash into real estate holdings to preserve it. I believe this path is low risk with high reward, and when it comes to investing in anything, those are the two things I always look for.

Real Estate Strategies for Success

In this strategies for success session, we'll talk about two aspects of real estate investing. The first portion will cover income strategies, which is what we just talked about. These are strategies for securing and purchasing passive income generating real estate. The second portion will talk about capital gains strategies. With these strategies you will be able to do short term real estate deals for quick profits, not cash flow. These activities will further accelerate your wealth accumulation so you can purchase your next long term income property and grow your passive income.

Calculating Your ROI

Most people purchase real estate based on two things, emotions and numbers. When people buy real estate based on the property, they are buying on emotion. They look at the curb appeal, the decor and the features of a property. Investors, however, purchase based on the numbers. They are not buying based on the property itself, they are buying based on the deal. For example, say an investor comes across a potential property that is listed on the MLS. It can be a horrible investment today, but a great one tomorrow. The only difference being that the seller lowers the price tomorrow. As a real estate investor, it should be all about the deal, not emotions.

The cap rate, or capitalization rate, is a percentage figure that is often shown on property listings. Many people confuse this with the ROI, the return on investment. They think that purchasing a property with a 10% cap rate means that they are earning a 10% return on their investment if they buy the property.

Cap Rate

Net Operating Income (gross income - expenses) divided by Selling Price.

A property that generates a $35,000 net operating income per year, selling at $500,000, has a cap rate of 7%. This figure is used as a benchmark to determine the value of similar properties in the same market. For example, if you know how much income a property nets, and you know that similar properties in the area are known to sell at certain cap rates, then you can find out what a property is truly worth. Using the above example, let's say you see a very similar property down the street that is selling at $400,000. The property looks to be of similar style and age, but it only has $23,000 in net operating income. 23,000/400,000 = 0.0575 = 5.75% cap rate. That sounds low if other similar properties are selling at a 7% cap rate. Based on that information, you should ask the seller why they are not pricing the property closer to $328,571 (23,000 / 7%), which is what it is worth based on the numbers.

The cap rate is primarily used to determine the value of a property, not your actual return on investment. The difference between this figure and your true ROI is that the cap rate is based on the property being fully paid off. In real world scenarios, that is rarely the case. A property with a 7% cap rate can be a good investment or a bad one depending how you structure the deal, such as the amount of down payment you invest and other loan terms. It can turn out to be a cash cow or a money sucker, all depending on what your cash on cash return looks like.

Cash on Cash Return

The cash on cash return gives you a better idea of your true return on investment. It takes into account how much money you invest in the property (down payment), and the cost to service that debt (mortgage payments and interest). Let's take a look at three different scenarios based on the same hypothetical $500,000 property with a 7% cap rate.

Example 1 (All cash deal)

Gross Income	$100,000
Operating expenses	($65,000)
Net Operating Income	$35,000
Total Investment (all cash)	$500,000

Cash on Cash return = 35000 / 500000 = 0.07 = **7%**

Example 2 (Financing Deal)

Net Operating Income	$35,000
Debt Service (6% Interest only)	$24,000
Net Cash Flow	$11,000
Total Investment (20% down)	$100,000

Cash on Cash return = 11,000 / 100000 = 0.11 = **11%**

Example 3 (Highly Leveraged Deal)

Net Operating Income $35,000

Debt Service (8% Interest only) $36,000

Net Cash Flow   ($1000)

Total Investment (10% down) $50,000

Cash on Cash return = -1000 / 50000 = -0.02 = **-2%**

In these three examples, you can see the difference between a cap rate and the cash on cash return. The cap rate is identical in all three cases, but the return on investment is very different. It also shows the power and risks of leverage. By financing a portion of the deal, the investor in this example would increase his ROI by 4% and earn 11% return per year. However, in a highly leveraged deal where the investor only puts down 10% as a down payment, that same property would generate a negative 2% annual return. With a lower down payment, the investor would often have third party investors as well as traditional financing, bumping his debt service cost to something like 8% average or higher. In this example, the investor would have to come out of pocket $1000 per year just to cover all expenses. The investor turned out to be a gambler.

The cash on cash return is not perfect, but it produces the best picture of your real world cashflow and return on investment. In the real world, you would have to take into account tax effects, amortization (a reduction in the loan principle), changes in future income or expenses, and costs associated with the eventual exit strategy. That being said, the cash on cash return calculation is still the best way to determine whether or not a deal is worth your time and money.

The Best Time To Buy

While it is true that great deals are made every single day, your probability of landing great deals is higher during bad times and lower during good times. Most human beings naturally have a herd mentality. Both euphoria and despair are highly contagious. You see examples of this in many things from music to clothing, smartphones, social media and sales like Black Friday. When everyone is doing something, our brain tells us that it must be good. If you walk down the block and everyone starts looking up, you'll likely do the same. Unfortunately, this tendency is your enemy when it comes to investing or buying anything. Not surprisingly, your immediate circle will give you encouragement to invest in or buy a house when times are good. They will question and doubt your decision to buy when times are bad. That is how ordinary people think. It is the extraordinary ones who go out and build fortunes during tough times. If you don't remember anything else when it comes to investments, remember Warren Buffett's famous words: "Be fearful when others are greedy and be greedy when others are fearful."

When it comes to real estate, buying property when times are good is an emotional act. It is easy to invest during the good times. Everyone is optimistic. The headlines are reporting good news in the economy and in the housing sector. Other people are making investments. You've got money to invest, and that annoying fear of missing out sets in. Despite all the wonderful headlines, what we generally see during good times are higher prices, increased buyer competition, lower inventories, and less time on the market. All of these big picture factors will lower your probability of finding a good deal. If you're a seller then you'll love these good times.

While it is easy to invest when times are good, it is often very difficult to invest during bad times. It requires conviction and courage to go against the herd. It requires unwavering discipline to take a risk when everyone else thinks the sky is falling and that things will go from bad to worse. Even banks are scared to lend money during tough times. Loans will be harder to obtain. But remember the saying: "the harder the battle, the sweeter the victory." Investing when times are bad is an act based on intelligence, not emotion. Through knowledge, you'll recognize that during bad times you will see lower prices, higher inventory, less competition and longer durations on the market. These factors set up an environment for savvy new investors to get rich.

Creating a fortune during bad times is not due to lower asking prices alone. The primary reason that fortunes are made is sellers' willingness to negotiate. In a previous example, we talked about a hypothetical $500,000 property that would generate a cash on cash return of 11%. If that same property was sold during bad times but negotiated down to $400,000, it increases your cash on cash return to 17%. With only a 20% reduction in the selling price, the cash on cash return went up by a whopping 55%. That change in ROI accelerates you wealth growth and increases cash flow significantly. You see, during good times there is a lot more competition amongst buyers and properties are selling fast. Sellers have no reason to negotiate. They know that another buyer is just around the corner so they have a "take it or leave it" mentality. During bad times, however, there are not a lot of buyers and there are usually more properties for sale as sellers deal with hard times themselves.

Due to increased supply and decreased demand, properties will be selling slower. Sellers know that the longer the property stays on the market, the longer it'll take to get out of their predicament. They, along with everyone else will be thinking that things will go from bad to worse. These people are reacting based on emotion. When you invest with intelligence during tough times, you are using the sellers' emotional states against them. When you make offers, you'll be able to say "take it or leave it." More often than not, you will land a much better deal when you find a motivated seller.

Research The Market

When it comes to property, you should never limit yourself to the city or region that you live in and are familiar with. Many times it won't make sense to do so. Successful investors will research and develop a list of potential regions that provide sustainable rents as well as possible growth. Nowadays, information is easy to come by. Websites like city-data.com provide an incredible amount of stats on cities and their communities. The primary factors that you should look at when researching potential markets are value, employment, and population growth.

The market that you are considering investing in should provide value to both you and potential renters. It should never be about price alone. There are plenty of areas in the United States with extremely low-priced real estate that still offer little value. They'll likely be in the middle of nowhere with low demand for rentals. To determine the value of a market to you as an investor, you can look at the listings and past sales of investment properties in the area. What are the usual cap rates? A low priced area that also sells with low cap rates offers little value to you. Secondly, you have to ask what value does the market provide to the renter? The more scarce and expensive houses are in the area, the more value people will find in renting. If homes are abundant and very affordable, there is little reason for someone to rent rather than buy.

To better determine the affordability of homes in the area, we must not look at home prices alone. We need the other part of the equation, which is income. This is why the second factor to look at is employment. What is the average income in the area? What types of jobs are they? Is it a rural area with mostly farming jobs or is it the next Silicon Valley? Knowing these factors, you can get an idea of how easy it is to purchase a home in the area. The easier it is to purchase, the less demand there is for rentals.

While we look at employment, you'll also want to get an idea of the long-term sustainability of the market. Find out what the unemployment rate is and how it compares to other cities and the nation as a whole. If there is higher than average unemployment, that may tell you that the area is on the decline. If unemployment is low, the next thing you want to look at is the diversity of the local economy. Ideally you'll want to invest in an area that has various industries that are employing people. I always look for areas that have thriving medical, energy, technology, and manufacturing sectors. Try to avoid areas that are dependent on a single industry or employer. A diverse local economy will give the area more resilience when one sector is on the decline nationwide.

To get an idea of job growth in the potential market, we can look at data as well. We can look at the job growth rate and how it compares to other cities. To get a more specific idea of future job growth, it is wise to research current and future large development projects in the area. You'll want to look at everything from infrastructure such as freeway expansions to sporting venues like stadiums. Look for news about the development of malls, schools and hospitals. If these projects are planned or underway, then you are leveraging the expensive research that these giant entities have already conducted. These types of projects all point to future job growth in the area.

The last factor we want to consider is population growth. Surely we'd want to invest in an area that people are moving to. A strong local economy and job growth would be a good reason for people to move. However, we should also study the psychology of future homebuyers as well. Put yourself in the shoes of potential buyers and think as if you are moving to the area you are researching. Look for amenities, local activities, weather, and culture. Think about what the next generation of homebuyers will want in an area. Personally, I only invest in areas that I wouldn't mind living in myself. With this covered as well, then you have the potential for future appreciation in addition to cashflow.

Research The Neighborhood

After you've done your research on potential markets to invest in, its time to research on a micro level. You'll want to weed out certain neighborhoods and focus on looking at property at just a handful of them. You'll be able to find a lot of data on crime from crimereports.com. They have an excellent interface that puts everything onto a map so you can visually see which areas to avoid. It is also definitely worth your while to talk to actual people who live in the city or the region to find out which areas are worth investing in. Keep in mind however, that some residents don't want investors to come into their areas because they think we will drive up prices and rent to bad people. So when dealing with residents, you should present yourself as a potential buyer who is moving a family to the area.

To contact actual "boots on the ground", the easiest way is to participate in online forums. I will typically do a

Google search for "best neighborhoods in _____" and see what comes up. If I don't find specific enough information, I will then search for forums dedicated to residents of specific cities. I would join the forum, introduce myself and start asking questions. I did this for the city of Elk Grove, CA as well as Austin, TX and Syracuse, NY. Many people who are active on these types of forums are willing to help in any way they can and they tend to be the type of people who know exactly what goes on in certain areas. Your mission here is to find out things about crime, employment, schools, and accessibility of certain neighborhoods from people who live in the city themselves.

The next step in narrowing down your search would be to actually travel to the area and spend a weekend there. I've done this many times and it is the only way to truly get a feel for the area. During this visit, you can take the opportunity to meet with a knowledgeable, experienced realtor that specializes in helping investors secure properties. I prefer to work with realtors who own rental properties themselves. It is also wise to interview potential property managers. Property managers will have a wealth of knowledge about the different neighborhoods in the area. They are running the day-today operations, so it is vital to get their take. While visiting, check out the local businesses close to where you want to invest and talk to people. You'll get a clear picture of the people who live and work in the area.

Research The Property

Once you've narrowed down the actual neighborhoods that you want to invest in, then it is time to look at potential properties. A good way to find newly listed or even unlisted opportunities is to sign up for newsletters. Most realtors who specialize in investment property will have a website set up with only investment properties for sale with an option to join their buyer's list. Even if you have a dedicated agent already, signing up for these newsletters will give you first knowledge of new listings that may not have even hit the market yet. Secondly, you can sign up to get alerts on the local MLS once new properties or price adjustments are made in those neighborhoods.

When making your offer, use the cap rate to determine the fair market value of the property. If you're offering a lower than asking price, either make sure it's a buyer's market in the area or make sure you have a valid reason. For example, if the property is visually in poor condition, a reduction in price could be justified in order to cover repair work. Once the property is in contract, that's when the real digging begins. Many investors will tell you that the real negotiation starts after the sales contract is signed.

On most real estate transactions, you are granted a due diligence period after the initial sales contract is signed. This is when you will obtain inspections, geologist reports, and other documentation that will provide insight that cannot be seen by yourself. It is also important to verify the numbers used to calculate the cap rate. Sellers and agents are known to be very liberal with the numbers. On some pro-forma forms, they'll use numbers based on how the property will perform in the future, not how it is currently performing or how it has performed in the past. You should verify the cost of expenses as well as the rent amounts and vacancy rate.

During this due diligence period, it is wise to seek the opinion of a property manager or company that you will be hiring. Some may come out for free while others may charge a consulting fee. The property manager will determine if the rents are realistic and how easy it will be to fill vacancies. They have direct knowledge of what tenants look for and what certain type of properties can rent for.

Another specialist to consult with is the contractor or handyman that will be performing maintenance on the property after you take ownership. This person will give you an idea of the scope of work that the property currently needs and what to expect going forward in terms of maintenance. The big things to look for are existing or potential problems with electrical, plumbing, HVAC, the foundation and the roof. These are all very costly repairs that you'll want to avoid.

Should anything major come up during the due diligence period such as incorrect expense numbers or significant repairs required, the selling price is oftentimes re-negotiated with the seller. Keep in mind that the seller is not obligated to lower the price. However, unless it is a pure seller's market or there is a backup offer, the seller should concede in an effort to close the deal.

Finding and Creating Value

Solid cashflow is generated by purchasing good rental properties, but fortunes are created by finding and creating value. Finding or creating value is achieved by increasing future revenue, decreasing future expenses, or decreasing the purchase price. It is often said that the money is made going into the deal. Good investors never depend on property appreciation; that's just a bonus. The bulk of the future profit is captured when the investor identifies hidden value in a property.

First, you can create value by identifying properties that are either not utilizing or underutilizing revenue streams. The most obvious example is rents that are significantly under market value. This occurs for many reasons. Sometimes the property owner is a mom and pop operator who just keeps the rent the same for years rather than keeping up with market rents and dealing with vacancies. Another reason is due to the condition of the exterior or interior of the building. In these cases, your property manager should be able to advise you on the potential increase in rent the unit can generate if it was updated. The contractor can let you know what those updates would cost and if there is a more efficient alternative. Another way to increase revenue would be to add new forms of revenue. Are there garages that could be rented out? Is there an area that can be turned into a coin operated laundry room? Perhaps the lot is even big enough for further development to add additional units.

The only limit is your imagination, creativity, and willingness to pursue.

The second way to create value is to identify expenses of a potential property that can be significantly reduced. If the property is accumulating recurring maintenance expenses with a particular system such as plumbing, HVAC or electrical, determine if there is a way to solve the issue by refurbishing or replacing the system. Then see if the seller will pay for that expense. See if appliances simply need replacing rather than constant repairs. If there's a high turnover rate, talk to the tenants and current property manager to find out what is causing it. Perhaps the property is attracting unpleasant loitering. Perhaps cars are getting broken into at night. Sometimes these things can be solved simply by installing high efficiency exterior lighting as well as cameras. In one of my parents' properties, we had an issue with unwanted cars parking in the lot so we simply installed a gate in the entrance that only tenants were able to open. The problem was instantly resolved.

Another big expense is simply mismanagement. If an incompetent property manager is in charge of leasing vacant units, it'll take them twice the time it should to get it rented. If they fail to address tenant problems, the tenant will surely leave. If the contractor is incompetent or simply a thief, your maintenance cost is drastically higher. Mismanagement can mean thousands of dollars in extra vacancy and maintenance expenses per year. Identifying mis-managed property is a surefire way to create value going into the deal.

Lastly, you can create value simply by not buying your investment properties at retail price. Many successful investors will agree that the best deals are often not found on the market. When you're a Phase 3 entrepreneur in search of real estate deals, let everyone know that you are a property investor. Everyone in your circle should know that you are looking to buy. This opens up the door for incredible deals to be made, especially with motivated sellers of mismanaged properties. Once you build a name for yourself, you can take this inactive approach to buying properties below retail. Somehow deals seem to come to you.

When you're starting out, however, you'll have to take a proactive approach to finding deals below retail. Once you've established a market and several neighborhoods within that market, hunt for distressed properties. Many of them will show visual signs of distress. It may not be updated and maintenance will be at a minimal. Identify these properties and start digging for ownership information. Almost all data is public information and either you or your broker can find out about the story behind the property. You can find out who the owner is and contact them. You can find out when they bought it, how much they owe on the property and much more. Ideally, you'll want to come across an owner who purchased the property at a low price, doesn't owe much and has owned it for quite a long time. The lack of maintenance may show that the owner no longer has the interest or energy to update the property. If the seller purchased the property a long time ago at a low price, you'll have a better chance of scoring a great price since they will be profitable nonetheless. On the other hand, if the property was purchased at a high price or the owner owes a lot on the property, then it will likely be tough for them to sell at a low price even if they wanted to.

Another strategy for finding great deals is to hunt for expired listings. These are properties that have been on the market for so long that they are now off the market. What you want to find out is why the property didn't sell. Remember earlier when we talked about ROI. The difference between a bad deal and a good deal is often times just a matter of price. The selling price will change the ROI drastically one way or the other. If the unsold property has good potential but just needs some work, contact the seller to see if they are willing to accept a lower price. At that time they have no leverage in the negotiation so unless they are incredibly stubborn, they will probably be willing to rethink the selling price in an effort to sell the property. They already tried it their way and it didn't work.

Build a Team

Real estate is a team sport, and to win in this game, you can't just have any team. You need a team of lions! If you settle for anyone and put them on your team, you're bound to have some cubs. These people will do as they're told, tell you what you want to hear and think well within the box. Sometimes if you're not careful, you may even let a few snakes into your team. Pick and choose your people wisely. Here are some people who are vital to your real estate team.

Broker

Brokers and agents are a dime a dozen. Many are

simply sales people treating the job as just another gig while others live and breathe real estate. All brokers send you listings and show properties, but remember that this person represents you in negotiations as well. They need to be able to efficiently communicate price justifications on your offer and they need to know how to use leverage during the due diligence process. I prefer to deal with brokers who are investors themselves. They don't get emotional and they'll tend to give you straightforward answers.

Property Manager

The property management company or individual manager will make or break you. While the broker represents you during the sale, the manager represents you after the sale. They deal with tenants and contractors. The ideal characteristics of a property manager are someone who is honest, customer service driven, but is also tough. You want your tenants to be taken care of but you don't want them to walk all over the manager. Be sure to obtain references from both property owners as well as tenants at properties that the company manages.

Contractor

Your contractor or handyman will be vital throughout the duration of your ownership. They need to be timely, efficient and honest. Some contractors are shortsighted. They take advantage of the situation and want to hose you, thinking you'll come back for more later. Explain to a contractor upfront that you expect quality, efficient work at fair prices in exchange for years of loyal business on multiple properties.

Accountant

It's not how much you make, it's how much you keep. Your accountant is your first line of defense against unnecessary taxes. Find someone who will think outside the box and find ways to minimize your tax liabilities. Accountants are a dime a dozen, but a good accountant is priceless. Do your homework and don't be afraid to ask questions and get referrals.

Insurance Agent

An often-overlooked member of your team is the insurance agent. Don't think of this as someone you call just when you have to buy insurance. Don't just stick with a default agent that the company assigns to you. This person should be treated as a valuable member of your team because they find the best ways to protect your interests while keeping your insurance expenses to a minimum. These people are also commonly found, but those who think outside the box and work to keep you as a long-term customer are rare.

Build a Business

While income and wealth preservation may be all you originally wanted when you first get into real estate, the endeavor will soon morph into a full-blown business. As your success and experience grows, your team will inevitably get stronger. You will attract cash investors and potential deals will present themselves more often than when you first start. A real estate investment business often includes more hands-on projects such as rehabbing and turnkey deals or fast profit deals such as wholesaling. These strategies are primarily for capital gains, not income. Like stock market trading, taking advantage of short-term capital gain opportunities in real estate will allow you to build your portfolio of income generating properties faster by helping you accumulate capital.

Rehabbing

Rehabbing is very popular these days. It has been glamorized by reality TV shows. During the real estate boom, almost everyone was doing it. It was foolproof because property appreciation made up for incompetence. Rehabbing involves the purchase of property that is in need of repairs and updates. The property is then resold at a higher price after being repaired, updated, and staged. It is better to get into rehabbing after years of experience in owning property. This is because you don't have a solid, trustworthy team when you first start out. When you have a competent team of lions, your information is more precise and thus your risk is reduced. Your broker will know what the property will sell for after it is rehabbed. Your contractor will tell you exactly what it will cost and how long it will take to do the rehab work. Your network of investors will be there to put in the cash so you can minimize your own investment for acquisition and holding costs. Getting into rehabbing after you have an established team is a great way to generate more profits so you can purchase that next income property sooner.

Turnkey Deals

Turnkey deals are when you purchase undervalued properties, fix them up, lease it out and sell the finished package to another investor. You may not want to keep the property for a variety of reasons. Maybe it's too small a property or it's located in an area that you don't like. The fact is your broker will come across these types of properties and the profit will be too tempting to ignore. After your contractor team fixes up the property, your property manager leases it out and your broker sells it to another investor. Certain Investors, especially new ones, love turnkey deals because all of the work has already been done. They can invest their money and start receiving checks the month right after closing. You can easily profit from this growing demand.

Wholesaling

From time to time, you may come across real estate wholesaling opportunities. Wholesaling is when you find a flipping opportunity for another investor or team. What happens is once you become known as a property investor and rehab specialist, people will come to you to sell you their junk properties. That, or you can find them on your own. However with wholesaling, instead of doing the rehab and flip yourself, you get another investor or team to do it. The reasons for this are simple. Maybe your resources are already tied up in other projects, your contractors are too busy or you simply want to go on a vacation and don't want to do the whole rehab deal.

In the wholesaling process, you'll first lock up a deal with the seller of the property at an agreed upon-price. For example you lock up a contract for a certain number of days for a property at a price of $200,000. You estimate that it needs $30,000 worth of work but after that it will sell for $300,000. You would then contact your network of other investors or brokers and let them know you have a complete rehab project available for $210,000 needing $30,000 of work with a market value of $300,000 after repairs. You would then assign the contract to the investor who will take on the rehab project. In this case, you would make a $10,000 profit in a short amount of time while putting up almost no money of your own. Wholesaling is yet another money generating tool in your investment arsenal.

Start Your Seven Figure Life
Wealth Journey

"If you are willing to do only what is easy, life will be hard. But if you are willing to do what's hard, life will be easy."
-T. Harv Eker

The path of becoming financially free using the internet is pretty simple. You start a business, grow it, run it from wherever you want, and invest the difference. Learn and perfect stock trading strategies. Accumulate wealth while living life on your own terms, then preserve that wealth by investing in real estate and receiving passive income. Retire from your businesses whenever you feel like it. You see, the path to wealth is as simple as that. It is literally a few sentences. However, applying it is far from easy. The thing is you have to actually do it. That is where most people give up. They look for short cuts. A lot of people are not willing to push themselves and do the work for their own future but they are ready and willing to do the work to get someone else rich in exchange for a paycheck. Success isn't some radical or highly intellectual concept that only the gifted or privileged can achieve. Anyone with the desire, discipline, and dedication will achieve success and great wealth. It is *simple* but it is not *easy*.

The two primary internet business models I went over are tried and true. It doesn't involve any new moneymaking "system" or get rick quick schemes. It involves building a real business and a brand that is sustainable and scalable. This will be your foundation, your primary moneymaker that sets you up to be able to invest and build wealth. Phase 1 of the wealth building journey determines whether you are destined for greatness or mediocrity. It is important that during this phase you never give up. Don't confuse failing with giving up. Failing simply means that you tried something and it didn't work. Ask any entrepreneur about their failures and they'll have a list of them. You'll learn from failure and you'll become a better version of yourself. Giving up is permanent. I don't like the saying that goes, "failure is not an option". Of course failure is an option. If you got into the wrong job, business or investment, would you keep wasting time and money on it or would you cut your losses and move on to something with more potential? In the ten plus years that I've been building and running my internet businesses, I can remember about ten that were complete failures. I cut my losses and moved on. The key is that even though

I failed, I learned, grew and never gave up on the big picture.

10 Rules for a Successful Business

Every business is different, but there are certain fundamentals that give you the best chance of success. I've gathered these 10 rules from my own experience and from other multi-millionaire online entrepreneurs.

1. Research thoroughly. Many internet marketers will talk about researching keywords and trying to find unexploited niches that you can break into to make money. While I still do that to see the search volume and general trends, I don't think this is nearly as important as it once was. You're not going to find some secret niche topic or product. The internet has become crowded, but you can still make a lot of money in a crowded space. What's important is that you research the market, products or topics and see if it <u>fits you</u>. Do you believe in it, are you passionate about it? Can you get excited about it for years? Find the competitors. Pinpoint the successful ones and get an idea of how they sell, how they market and how the promote themselves. Determine if that fits your personality type. This is more important than finding some secret unexploited niche because the niche

doesn't determine your success, whether or not you can sell it does.

2. This ties into #1. I think it is very important these days to make yourself the face of the brand or business. There has to be a story behind the brand. With the flooded internet, trust and attention is scarce. At the end of the day, people buy from people. Small is the new big, the personal touch adds credibility and that leads to sales. I'm naturally reserved and I prefer to speak less than I know and have more than I show. Yet when it comes to business I still force myself to add personality to my businesses and social media channels. I put myself out there on SevenFigureLife.com with full transparency. At first I wasn't comfortable with it, but I know that's what I had to do to reach as many people as possible. Dreams are never attained by staying in your comfort zone.

In his commencement speech at Stanford University, Steve Jobs said, "Almost everything, all external expectations, all pride, all fear of embarrassment or failure, these things just fall away in the face of death, leaving only what is truly important. Remembering that you are going to die is the best way I know to avoid the trap of thinking you have something to lose." I know it sounds dramatic and out there, but it's so true that's why I like this quote so much. In the big picture, none of this matters. So what is there to be afraid of? Be the rock star of your business. Push your limits and keep stepping out of your comfort zone.

3. Be different. Find an angle or some way to differentiate your product or marketing approach. The saying "there's nothing new under the sun" holds true even for online businesses. Many people are selling the same stuff, the same ideas, the same education but with their own twist or catering to a different target audience. Find your most successful competitors and brainstorm about how you can do things differently to set your business apart. Eric Thomas is known as ET the hip hop preacher. He's a motivational speaker that has the uncanny ability to reach younger audiences with his personal story and oratory skills. The material isn't revolutionary, most are timeless truths. But he is different and he reaches a different core audience. Because of that he has amassed a huge following. I watch his Youtube videos every week. You don't have to re-invent the wheel, you just need a unique way to sell it.

4. Set daily, weekly and monthly rituals and execute them. I don't call these things goals because goals mean you are trying to do something. As Tony Robbins once said, you need to develop *rituals*. The single reason people have for not doing something is that they forgot. Nowadays with smartphones that have reminders, that's no longer a valid excuse. Set reminders and do not do anything else until you complete a task. Daily rituals may be adding products, posting to social media, and connecting with others in your industry. Weekly rituals can include content creation and research. Monthly rituals include sending out newsletters, evaluating your marketing efforts and making adjustments. Set these up and make sure you do them. This is more important than the idea itself, how your website looks, going out with friends, watching sports, etc.

5. Outsource. You will never be able to do everything alone, nor should you want to. For highly technical and tedious tasks you definitely want to pay others to do it. With an army of local and overseas providers at your service, it is easier than ever to get good work at low prices from sites like Upwork.com. I have been using them (formerly known as Elance) for over 10

years. It is definitely one of the best ways to leverage your time and scale your operation.

While it may take time to find good freelancers, the sooner you start the sooner you can find those dependable people. With my team that I have built, the majority of tedious tasks are no longer handled by myself. Unlike with traditional brick and mortar businesses, I don't have to take these people on as employees and incur that additional expense, taxes and liability. Freelancers are only paid for the time they spend working and nothing else and you can replace poor performing freelancers within days.

6. Focus on free marketing first. There are so many sources of free traffic these days, primarily from social media. These platforms let you reach your customers directly and talk directly to them. Never before was this possible. Develop a solid content marketing strategy that builds your following and gets you free traffic. Before you start throwing money at advertising, exhaust all of the ideas you have that will bring you free traffic. Once you gain traction, use sponsorships and paid advertisements to supplement that growth.

7. It is hard to become successful alone. With both e-commerce or a blog business, no person is an island. To grow, you need the help or others who have decent reach. Systematically network with other people in your industry or influencers in your market. Develop joint ventures that can benefit the both of you as well as their audience. Ask your customers to help promote you and spread the word. Give them incentives such as a free gift, a discount or free shipping on future orders to share your business with their network. As much as you have to do your part in business, you must also seek outside help so your company can grow at a much faster rate.

8. When a marketing opportunity comes to you, put up your guard. Throughout my years, I've learned one thing when it comes to marketing. No beneficial marketing opportunity has ever come to me, it was always the other way around. If you're getting emails about SEO service offers, sponsorships, featuring your products on TV, etc., put up your guard. I have encountered tons of scams over the years, one of which actually cost me around $4000. Just remember one thing. You're the one that needs traffic, you're the one that needs the reach, so why would someone

with those things solicit you and not the other way around? Maybe not all spam emails are from bad people, but to me, if they are that desperate they are not worth my time or money anyway. Plus, whatever audience they do have will be likely saturated with ads since they are going around soliciting everyone for ad money.

9. Persistence and work ethic is the difference between success and failure. I find this to be true in anything from fitness to business. It's not just about the idea or the market you are in. Showing up and simply doing what you say you will do is half the battle. Some people may have rich parents or know the right people, but the great equalizer is time. Everyone has 24 hours in a day and the one thing you can control is your ability to outwork your competition. Remember, do what they won't and in the future you can do what they can't. We often associate success with extravagant lifestyles like nice cars, travel, watches, designer clothing etc. What we don't see is the hours of working late night, the lack of sleep, the uncomfortable phone calls and meetings, and the countless failures. It's not just luck that makes people rich. Some say the harder you work, the luckier you

get. If you can only use 1 rule out of 10, this one will be it. As Arnold Schwarzenegger said, "Leave no stone unturned. You never want to fail because you didn't work hard enough."

10. Know when to cut losses. This is a skill that takes time to develop, both in your business and investments. There is the fine line between persistence and an exit strategy. You don't want to fail too early but at the same time you don't want to waste your time and resources on something that just isn't going to work. In those cases it's better to move on to something that will work sooner rather than later. To determine if its time to cut losses, I would evaluate two things: did you work and did the business work? Traffic and conversions has a lot to do with 'did you work'. Did you do all of your daily, weekly and monthly tasks? Did you fully implement your strategies? Were you persistent in following up with influencers? Only you know if you gave it 100%. If you haven't, then you haven't done your part yet, therefore it's not time to cut losses.

If you believe you gave it all you had, 100% for months and months and you're not seeing results, then it's time to see if the business is working. Trace back the entire timeline of the journey from initial concept and research to the content and marketing strategy. Pinpoint areas that you may have had incorrect assumptions about. Solicit feedback from past customers. Contact influencers that you networked with. If they weren't willing to promote your business, ask why. Once you pinpoint flaws in the business concept itself, you can decide if it's feasible and worth your time to adjust, or to have to cut losses and move on to something else. Following tip #1 will minimize your odds of having to use tip #10. However, if you remember from earlier in the book, failing is not the same as giving up. Failures are lessons, stepping stones in the journey of a successful entrepreneur. Knowing when to cut losses is actually a great business skill to possess.

What I leave you with

At the time of this writing, I am at the Riu Palace resort in Cabo San Lucas, relaxing on my balcony and overlooking the pristine pacific ocean. The cool breeze against the warm, slightly humid weather completes this dream-like scene. My businesses and investments are generating income while I'm away. This morning, I spent about 30 minutes catching up on emails. I also closed a trade I had on the SP500 index (symbol SPX) to take safe profits of about $800, just so I don't have to look at it for the rest of the week. Parts of this book were written on cruise ships such as the *Oasis of the Seas* and the *Allure of the Seas*, sister ships that are currently the largest in the world. The top 10 tips were written in while my wife and I sailed Asia, onboard the *Quantum of the Seas*, one of the newest cruise ships in the world. I have written chapters and made revisions from world class hotels in many different cities and countries, local beaches and cafes, my favorite lunch spots and many times just at home where I have a gorgeous view of San Francisco, lush mountains and the bay. My businesses and investments have given me the ultimate time freedom.

Yes, this lifestyle comes with financial abundance as well. As my businesses grew, I have been able to buy all the material goods that I need and then some. I have a passion for items with meticulous engineering and craftsmanship, such as watches, cars, and art. I have been able to treat my parents, both in-laws, my wife and my sister with trips, Rolex watches and other luxury goods. I was blessed to be able to give my dad a brand new Lexus for his birthday, free and clear. Though it shouldn't be all about material things, I think it is perfectly okay to be motivated by the finer things in life. After all, you only live once so why not strive to be the best version of yourself so you can experience the best that life has to offer? I'm a regular guy that grew up in an average middle class household. I live the Seven Figure Life thanks to technology, trial and error, and a never give up attitude. I have no doubt that if you choose to, you can live the lifestyle of your dreams.

Never be afraid to challenge conventional wisdom. Sometimes you have to take a step back and almost remove yourself from reality for a bit, in order to look at the world for what it is. You are here for a limited time and for how long no one knows. You will not live forever, so it is imperative that you break free and live life on your own terms. Modern society is set up so that the general public becomes chained to schools, jobs, and debt and then one day they die. You don't have to accept the world for what it is. We live in a time where you can easily live an unconventional lifestyle. Aside from technology, think about society and history as a whole. We're incredibly blessed to be living in this particular era. We have had ice ages, warlords, kings, slavery, plagues, tyrants, depressions, famine, communism and everything in between. Times are great compared to other points in history. You owe it to yourself and anyone depending on you to take advantage of these times and create a better life. The way to do that is to build a business that gives you more time and location freedom, all while you accumulate wealth to one day become financially free. That is how you escape this life course that someone else decided you were supposed to take.

The principles in this book are practically timeless. Though details might change, e-commerce is here to stay. People are buying online more than ever for the sake of convenience and cost savings. Expert bloggers will always be able to sell information that solves a problem then build a brand around that. The blog business model is growing and it is essentially replacing books, seminars, infomercials and instructional DVDs. The tools to help you become a better stock investor will never go away and the principles of technical analysis will never change. These things will only improve with technology. Real estate will always be a cash flow generating asset that preserves wealth because people will always need housing and land will only become more scarce with time.

It is time to decide that you truly want success and to take the first steps. Don't quit your job tomorrow, I'm not asking you to be reckless, but do start that business! Most people start and grow their business on the side. Get to brainstorming and just do it. "Someday" will turn into never. As I said time and time again, there is no better time to start than now. You can start a legitimate business with as little as an hour a day and very little money. Never at any other point in history would you be able to do that. Visit my blog www.SevenFigureLife.com. There you will find a comprehensive guide on starting your e-commerce or blog business. The guides are both completely free. My newsletter will send out monthly tips on internet marketing, business, investments, personal development and entrepreneurship.

Also, follow my journey on Instagram @SevenFigureLife for daily motivational content and updates. I'm also on Facebook at Facebook.com/SevenFigureOnline.

I sincerely hope that you start this journey now and follow through. I have spent many months writing this book for people like yourself. The biggest satisfaction I can get from this journey is for you to email me a year or two from now to tell me about your business and how your life has changed.

ABOUT THE AUTHOR

Danny Tsang is an entrepreneur, investor and blogger from San Francisco, CA. He has founded multiple successful jewelry brands as well as the luxury brand Seven Figure. His businesses have served hundreds of thousands of customers worldwide and generated millions of dollars in sales.

Through the Seven Figure Life blog, Danny has published articles and free training courses in the areas of E-Commerce, Blogging as a Business, Stock Trading, Real Estate Investing, and other areas of internet marketing.

Danny is constantly seeking to expand his business and investment portfolio and develop new ways to give back to the community of entrepreneurs. Be sure to keep up with the latest news, resources and developments at www.SevenFigureLife.com and follow him on Instagram @SevenFigureLife

SEVEN FIGURE

The premier luxury brand for success oriented
individuals.

www.SevenFigure.com

STAY MOTIVATED

Join the tens of thousands of like-minded people in our community. Follow me on social media for updates, insights, and exciting content posted daily.

@SevenFigureLife

Facebook.com/SevenFigureOnline

NOTES

www.ingramcontent.com/pod-product-compliance
Lightning Source LLC
Chambersburg PA
CBHW031929190326
41519CB00007B/461